Praise for *The 20time P* ...

"A compelling roadmap for motivating student innovation and complex problem solving."
—*Daniel H. Pink, author of* Drive *and* A Whole New Mind

"Kevin has his finger on the pulse of how technology is reshaping education and inspires thousands of other teachers to nurture a culture of curiosity and creativity."
—*Andrew McGonnigle, general manager of* TheGooru.com

"An illuminating example of how an educational paradigm shift can happen in the classroom and how one creative and entrepreneurial teacher can transform educational experiences. A great read and practical guide for all teachers who aspire for a new type of education for their students."
—*Yong Zhao, Ph.D., author of* World Class Learners: Educating Creative and Entrepreneurial Students

"In our rapidly changing world, it has become a moral imperative to help students become passionate lifelong learners, help them 'learn how to learn,' and empower them to change the world as they go. In my experience, 20time is the most effective way to do this. Kevin has been instrumental in inspiring educators from around the world to incorporate 20time in their classroom."
—Oliver Schinkten, *creator of* AssistEd Shift

"Kevin challenges educators to give students more freedom in planning their own time. This creates a classroom culture of independence, discovery and creativity, and challenges young people to think critically about how they can effect change in the world."
—*Cristin Frodella,* Google for Education *& creator of* Google Science Fair

The 20time Project

How educators can launch Google's formula for future-ready innovation

Kevin Brookhouser, M.Ed.

20time.org

To order additional copies of this book, visit 20time.org/book.

Interested in having Kevin speak to your group? Go to 20time.org/kevin.

To Sam.
May your life be full of curiosity
and opportunities to feed it.

You simply must do things.
—*Ray Bradbury*

Contents

Foreword

Mark Wagner, Ph.D.

President/CEO of EdTechTeam educational consultants
Director of the Google Teacher Academy, 2008 to 2011

We educators no longer live in a time when our job is to help students memorize a few things they might need someday. A smartphone and quick Google search are better suited to that task.

Our job is to prepare students for the future by helping them learn to access and use information in ways that are meaningful to them.

To tap into students' innate desire to learn about their world (and improve it), it's vital that we provide them the time and support necessary to pursue their own interests and passions. Offering students this time as part of their education tells them "you have all the resources of the school, including me, at your disposal," and asks them the most important question a teacher can ask:

"What do you want to learn?"

When I first started working as a high school English teacher in the late 1990s, I was lucky enough to work at a school committed to asking this question of every senior as part of a year-long project. We saw tremendous creativity, talent and skill emerge as students pursued cooking, video game programming, yoga, astronautics, and auto design. Even seemingly simple, non-challenging topics such as "learn about skateboards" would evolve by the end of the year into deep explorations of graphic design, retail sales and sports medicine.

I happened to teach both seniors and freshmen, and like many other teachers at the school, we found creative ways to offer a similar experience to younger students. Years later, I was finally able to give these approaches a name. I was working with Google staff to produce the Google Teacher Academy when they shared with me about 20 Percent Time, Google's practice of offering employees the hours and resources to develop passion projects on the side.

Since then, with teachers at all grade levels and in all subject areas, I've shared (or perhaps preached) the value of offering students 20time at school. That time could be delivered one day a week, one hour a day, or whatever works best. I've seen this type of program be successful in my wife's kindergarten class, with senior projects, and in every grade in between. I've also seen examples of this approach at work on every continent (except Antarctica).

One of my favorite examples is the Ignite Project at Albany Senior High School, just outside Auckland, New Zealand, where visionary school leadership made it possible to institutionalize 20 percent time as part of the school culture. All students spend their entire Wednesday working on a project pursuing one of their passions, and all the teachers are involved (three faculty mentors are required to sign off on each project before a student can begin). The students plant gardens, build windmills, film movies, restore cars, paint murals, produce software, and more. The evidence of their learning can be found everywhere at the school. These students have agency over their own learning, and they have a school with the courageous leadership and empowered teachers needed to make that happen.

But until now, there hasn't been a definitive resource available to guide educators and leaders interested in pursuing this path. In this inspiring volume, Kevin Brookhouser has generously shared the ways he's made 20 percent time work for his students in Monterey, California. He explains the big ideas underlying these types of projects, the intellectual and social impacts of the approach, and provides a step-by-step, concrete guide that makes it easy to build a successful program.

Kevin has made an invaluable contribution to our field and to all educators who want to ask their own students: *"What do you want to learn?"*

Acknowledgments

I've had more than a few parents approach me over the years exclaiming that their student's 20time Project has become a 100Time project, pulling them away from their other responsibilities. That happened to me with this book. I am so thankful for my favorite person in the world, **Beth**, for supporting this project the same year we were raising an infant. Love and thanks times infinity.

If you ever need help in a writing project, hunt down my editor, **Ria Megnin** (riamegnin.com). Sure, she's the most positive person I know, but she is also a hammer when something needs to get done accurately, precisely, and quickly. I am deeply grateful for her experience, compassion, and rigor. Can't wait to work with her on the next project.

We really tested the limits of collaborative technology while editing this thing, and I can't imagine how people did this before the miracle of Google Docs. Thanks to **Camilla Mann**, **Andrew Stillman**, and **Aaron Eden** for insightful use of the commenting feature to add clarity and spice to the copy.

Techsmith is without question my favorite software company, and not just because of their support for this book. Their incredible screencasting program, Camtasia, holds one of the very few app dock spots on my computer, nestled in there between Chrome and

Lightroom. With their tools, they are enabling teachers and students to create amazing images and videos, and they pay attention to teacher feedback. Ryan Eash at Techsmith knows that education software needs teacher feedback and is quick to respond. Teachers can create amazing things by starting at techsmith.com.

Rolling Hills Middle School is fortunate to have **Trisha Sanchez** as a 7th grade language arts teacher. She is one of the leading teachers applying the principles of 20time to her class. Trisha is also one of my top supporters in my Kickstarter campaign. Thank you, Trisha.

Kickstarter was an amazing platform for getting the backing I needed to get this project off the ground. I am so proud that this project was funded by people who believe in the value of 20time. I am so grateful to **all of you backers** for your support.

Finally, this book would truly not have been possible without the contributions of hundreds of my fellow educators, students, thinkers and leaders. I am part of an amazing community of teachers who share everything. I couldn't even begin to thank every person whose ideas are reflected in this book. Thanks to all of you on Twitter, Google Plus, Podcasts, Facebook, YouTube, and all those other places we meet to share ideas, break things and build something new.

The 20time Project

Introduction

My name is Kevin Brookhouser, and I love being a teacher in today's world.

Why today's world? Because of the extraordinary educational tools we have, and the extraordinary importance of how we use them to prepare students who are ready for the global challenges of the future.

I'm lucky to teach at York School in Monterey, California. This small, private school teaches students from all backgrounds in grades 8 to 12. It's a learning environment where I have tremendous support for exploring the edges of what's possible in education today—both in my classes and beyond.

For instance, since becoming a Google Certified Teacher and Google Education Trainer in 2010, I've incorporated many Google-created tools into my curriculum to transform learning spaces and experiences. I've also been given the opportunity to travel to conferences around the world, where I've spoken with thousands of teachers about the role of technology in education reform.

But tech tools aren't the most important thing I've learned from Google.

Since 2008, I've worked with the founders of the Google Teacher Academy, a group of schoolteachers who the company recognizes as education leaders. These inspiring people are active in moving the entire world of education forward, particularly through the use of technology in their classrooms.

The Academy brings teachers to Google's campus in Mountain View, California, where we learn about its culture. The goal is for us to take back some of the principles the company has learned about how the world works and apply them to education.

I love my work as a teacher too much to ever leave—even for Google—but I do give a lot of thought about what it would take to be hired there. Based on what I've seen, if I can prepare my students to be the kind of innovative, creative thinkers Google looks for, I'll have done my job of preparing them to be future ready.

"Future ready" has become a key focus of education circles worldwide. In 2008, the National Association of Independent Schools named me a Teacher of the Future. I worked with the charter team of 25 fellow Teachers of the Future from around the country to define what a classroom would look like that truly prepares young people for the challenges (and wonders) of the decades to come. Our community has grown considerably, and much of what we've learned informs the project-based learning approach I began using in my classroom in the fall of 2009.

In 2010, I joined fellow leading educators from around the world at an education conference in Bahrain. They included Gever Tulley, founder of The Tinkering School, whose TED Talk "5 Dangerous Things You Should Let Your Children Do" has deservedly drawn more than 3 million views, and Ewan McIntosh, whose No-Tosh Limited program helps schools develop innovative classrooms with collaborative, student-designed, project-based learning. Over the next few years, I met and worked with many other cutting-edge thinkers around the world, exploring how we can best prepare students to take on the big issues facing our world.

All this paid off in 2012, when the founder of the Google Teacher Academy, Mark Wagner, brought me on as a contributor to his new company, EdTechTeam. As their Student Agency Specialist, I get to travel around the world talking about future-ready education, helping school systems create the best possible learning environments using the latest technology and thinking available. It's an incredible joy to share what we're learning and meet the people my students are going to both compete with and collaborate with to solve our world's great problems.

One of my favorite aspects is how our work dovetails with 20time. EdTechTeam has found that six core pillars are needed in order for schools, teachers, and classrooms to effectively prepare students for the future:

1. Student agency

The first pillar of any future-ready educational environment is *student agency*. We've found that when we provide students with the opportunity to solve real-world problems through self-led projects, the students rise to standards higher than any teacher could propose. The added benefit? They're coming up with approaches and tools that can solve problems we adults haven't yet figured out how to tackle.

Most of this book will focus on how 20time fits this aspect of future-ready learning, but it's important to keep in mind the context that allows student agency to thrive. That context is provided by the remaining five pillars.

2. Teacher empowerment

Traditionally, the standards Western public school teachers had to follow have been intensely regimented and highly detailed. The truth is that in many developed nations (including the United States), teachers haven't been recognized as the professionals they are—professionals doing one of the most difficult jobs in the world. In many school districts, they're given almost no resources but asked to work miracles. And that's exactly what most teachers are doing.

Today's newer standards, including the Common Core, are more rigorous, but they offer far more flexibility in how teachers achieve their mandated goals. The standards actually give teachers more control over how they help students learn. That's a great move, because we've found that the more power we put in teachers' hands, the more good they can do. Teachers know what their students need. The biggest thing keeping most of them from delivering what's needed is having their hands tied by bureaucracy.

But things are finally shifting. We need to support that trend.

3. Inspiring spaces

Picture a classroom. What comes to mind? The first thing most of us think of is a square room with rows of desks facing a teacher's desk, probably with an apple, a blackboard and a set of books.

That's fine—if you're preparing students to work in factories. This traditional classroom space is the product of an industrial-era model of education. Just like factories, schools were designed to categorize students by age and (supposed) ability, then deliver curriculum in an assembly line format.

We're looking to transform the spaces in which students learn to encourage far more collaboration, creativity and student agency. When young learners are working together, they can focus on their work and their team rather than on the teacher. When they're given opportunities to be more mobile and even get out of the physical classroom, going out into the world to solve real-life problems, they learn even more through the experience.

One example of this is an exciting trend happening around the country: Schools are creating "maker spaces," essentially bringing back the old "shop." As traditional manufacturing jobs disappeared over the past 40 years, classes in industrial arts were cut from curriculums or farmed out to technical schools. But today, maker spaces allow students to learn many of the same essential skills. The difference is that they create their designs using 3-D printers, laser cutters and robotics. In the worldwide education renaissance under way, these spaces are frequently where the real change is happening.

I admit to some bias in wanting this trend to succeed. I remember the one woodworking class I took with tremendous fondness. Our teacher allowed us to act as entrepreneurs while we explored how to design, draft, build a team, create a budget, and manage both our materials and our safety. I learned more in that class than most of my others combined, and I still use those skills in training teachers, solving technical problems, designing websites, and looking for opportunities to serve others.

4. Courageous leadership

For any school or institution to move forward, education leaders must take risks. Education is historically very conservative, and its leaders are often entrenched in bureaucracy and slow to embrace change.

We need leaders who are willing to take the risks necessary to move at a pace that keeps up with the rest of the world. One of the most important things these leaders can do is give teachers the power to execute what they know is best for their students. It also means helping them discover and explore the latest tools and thinking happening in the education world.

5. Infrastructure

The workplaces of the future won't look like the schools of yesterday. Broadband Internet access is as essential to future-ready schools as electricity and plumbing. It's no longer a luxury, it's a human right.

All students need broadband Internet in order to have an education that connects them with their global world, provides opportunities to collaborate, and offers access to the infinite resources available online.

6. Hardware & software

Internet for a school is meaningless if students can't access it for more than a few minutes a week. Fortunately, the costs of both computers and applications are plummeting to near-zero.

For instance, Google Apps for Education, including amazing document collaboration and unlimited storage, is free for teachers and students. Adobe offers its creative suite of professional-grade graphic design, photo manipulation and movie editing tools for pennies a day. For $200, a student can get a Chromebook that gives them access to many of these tools.

As these tools become available, the challenge for educators is to help students learn to use them effectively and responsibly.

With all six pillars in place, we have a real chance to foster student agency in ways that prepare them to take on the challenges of the future.

Ways such as 20time.

The 20% Time Project

Every day I look at my news feed and see serious problems that are left unsolved. Climate change. Religious extremism. Poverty. Racism. Extinctions. Wars.

As a teacher, I'm optimistic that my students can solve these issues, but I know the same kind of high school education I received is not going to prepare them to do so.

Traditional education teaches students to solve problems for which we know the solutions. To do so, we teachers primarily use extrinsic motivators—rewards and punishments—in the form of grades. The truth is, these carrots and sticks don't encourage the innovative thinking required to create novel solutions for unsolved problems. In fact, as I'll explain, they undermine it.

So what motivates creative problem solving, instead? Two things: autonomy and purpose. Students need experiences where they have the freedom to learn what they want to learn about topics that have a purpose outside of the classroom. One of the best tools for doing so is project-based learning.

Google gets this. Embedded in Google's corporate culture is the concept of allowing engineers to take on independent projects not necessarily endorsed by management. This unofficial policy lets them invest 20 percent of their work time on self-led explorations to solve real problems. This is such a brilliant idea that when I first learned about it in 2007, I couldn't wait to bring it into my classroom as a way to make future-ready teaching a major part of the curriculum.

Sure enough, I've found that one of the most effective ways to boost student agency and promote the kind of world-changing, future-oriented thinking we need is to have students engage in a 20% Time Project. My classes spend the entire year devoting one period each week (and plenty more hours outside school) to independent projects the students themselves chose to pursue. They get lessons in entrepreneurship through giving project proposals and elevator pitches, make a significant difference in their chosen communities with tangible benefits, and wrap things up with a professional, open-to-the-community presentation complete with visuals, microphones and the all-important red carpet. And my students are "only" high school sophomores.

This book was written to help the many teachers, parents and colleagues who are eager to learn how to create a similar program for the young people in their lives. The first part explains why we need this kind of future-oriented education, and some of the learning philosophy underpinning the 20time project. Part Two is all about how to run a 20time program at your school—including how to avoid the many mistakes I made the first few times around. After that, I explore more about why 20time works, including the importance of embracing failure, providing audience-centered learning opportunities, and navigating academic curriculum standards.

A note about the term 20time: In my classroom and other project-based learning communities, we use the abbreviation 20time as shorthand for our 20% Time programs. You can find an entire learning community on Twitter built around the #20time hashtag.

It's amazing to be on the front lines of helping 20time projects unfold each year, and I know the impact goes far beyond the campuses of our schools. Thank you for being willing to learn more about this program and, perhaps, bring its benefits to more members of our most important generation: the ones who will shape our future.

Chapter I
We Need Wicked-Problem Solvers

If you're reading this book, you're someone who cares about the future. You're invested in helping the kids of today—toddlers, children, teenagers—grow into people who can shape the world into a better place.

You also understand what a challenge we're handing to them. We've created problems on a global level: environmental destruction, international terrorism, massive overconsumption alongside brutal poverty, cross-border trafficking of drugs and weapons and human beings, violence against women and minorities of every kind…

The list, of course, goes on. Many educators are in their professions because of this. Not because *we* know how to make the world a better place. But because we're confident solutions are out there, and we believe the best way to find them is through educating young people.

The question is, how? How do we create a generation capable of solving what earlier generations couldn't manage?

Formulas for survival

The issues we face in the interconnected society of the 21st century are so big and so complicated, they require a radically new, world-changing way of thinking about them.

This process starts by recognizing that problems come in two categories: *solved* and *unsolved*. Rhetoricians know these as algorithmic and heuristic problems.

From there, we can recognize that most educational systems are built around teaching algorithms. We show kids ways to solve problems that someone has already figured out. Then we make them show us they've learned the formulas, too.

Let me be clear: this teaching approach is not something to throw out. Passing down the knowledge gathered by our predecessors to the generations who follow provides the essential building blocks for our culture to survive.

Here's just a few examples:

—In math, we teach students how to use the Pythagorean theorem to solve the mystery of the length of the hypotenuse of a triangle, then use that information to design art pieces and buildings.

—In grammar, we help young people learn structures of language such as punctuation and spelling so they can better understand each other.

—In physics, we teach that force is the product of an object's mass times its acceleration, so students can solve equations about transportation and sports and more.

—In history, we share the formula called "balance of power." We explain and demonstrate how, when any one group appears to gain too much power, other groups team up to counter it. This helps students better understand strategies for predicting and coping with political and economic change.

Why we need new tools today

Our schools have a not-so-secret technique for transmitting these algorithms, these formulas representing the wisdom of the ages, into the young minds in our care:

Bribery.

For more than 150 years, Western educators have rewarded children with the help of extrinsic motivators, from good grades to field trips to opportunities for higher education. Some schools today even pay their high-performing students in cash or prizes.

We absolutely need people who understand the formulas and solutions that are the foundations of our culture, and bribery does encourage people to put in the work required to learn them. We know it works because we see bribes used effectively in the world every day, with people of all ages. Think about video games. Players who master a game's formula are rewarded. They get high scores, unlock achievements and more powerful game features, and (most important) get to play and experience more and more of the game. Social media does the same thing. The more you post, the more friends you attract. The more friends you attract, the more interesting content and connections you see. Then, of course, there are jobs. Ideally, people who show up and get the work done are the ones who get to keep coming back and keep receiving pay.

These are all bribes.

But there's plenty of debate about this use of bribery in education, especially regarding its darker half. The carrot-and-stick approach balances rewards with punishments including bad grades, letters sent home to parents, being held back a year. These punishments don't always fit the crimes, and too often doom creative, learning-disabled or underprivileged children to a life without choices.

Besides, bribing students to learn formula-based thinking can only take us so far. What happens when there's no formula to learn? No strategies that someone has already discovered?

Creating the thinkers of the future

To help students come up with totally novel solutions, we need educational experiences that let them explore *unsolved* or *heuristic problems*, such as homelessness, or the technology divide, or bridging cultural gaps.

That's where the 20% Time Project comes in. It's a tool for motivating innovation used by no less world-changing an organization than Google.

It's not written into any corporate management policy. But the culture at Google (and many other innovative companies) supports workers who see a need, come up with an idea, and want to dedicate 20 percent of their work time to pursuing it. Projects that succeed are brought to managers and given additional resources.

The results have been astounding. Many of Google's most popular and profitable offerings, including Gmail, Google News and AdSense, got their start as 20time side projects.

Google isn't the only company using this approach, of course. Some of the more famous include fellow Silicon Valley standout Hewlett-Packard and 3M, which pioneered 15% Time in the mid-20th century.

When brought into the classroom, 20time immerses young people in a kind of laboratory playground of unsolved problems. It creates a learning environment where they can develop the radical, transformative, unexpected thinking they, too, need to change the world.

In my classrooms at York School in Monterey, Calif., we've created just such a culture, investing a significant amount of time in project-based learning. They have wide latitude to come up with ideas, both in topic and scope. Of course, I place a tad more emphasis on management than Google does with its engineers. My students are required to produce a well-structured, year-long experiment in meeting some need for a specific audience or community.

Here are just a few examples of ideas these teens have pitched:
—Design a basketball program for 4th and 5th graders
—Teach local senior citizens how to use Facebook.
—Develop a website to help students with difficult math subjects.
—Experience life from a wheelchair for one month.
—Organize a benefit concert to collect books for a local library that burned down.
—Inspire gardening by planting a garden and blogging about the experience
—Use 3-D software to design an eco-friendly dream house
—Take photographs that help preserve local history

While some of these ideas may seem mundane, they're steps on the way to addressing larger, more wicked problems. Each of these proposals had the potential to help students develop skills in teaching, organizing, designing, empathizing, communicating, and connecting with different audiences—all of which are essential for tackling the major issues facing our world.

The 20time process

Leading a 20time Project doesn't stop with helping students generate workable ideas. Students crave, need and deserve both structure and guidance.

My students have to meet several major requirements over the course of their 20time projects. We'll explore these in detail in Part II of this book, but here are the core elements:

—Present a formal proposal to the class addressing the need for the project, the audience, the timeline of deliverables, the proposed tangible or digital results, the supplies and funding needed, and a summary that conveys their excitement.

—Create and maintain a blog tracking their project's development.

—As part of their mid-year exam, memorize and videorecord an elevator pitch for their work.

—For their final exam, deliver a five-minute memorized presentation describing their project and results. These are modeled after the talks given at TED conferences, complete with a projection screen and a red carpet.

In short, my students can't spend 20 percent of their year playing a video game and call that a win. I ask a lot more of them. They tend to struggle and fail and have to try again. And then they succeed at things none of us, including me, expected them to.

That's the whole point of 20time and other project-based learning approaches. The goal is not to give students school time and resources to play with a "passion project." It's not even about the positive community impact their projects might have. It's about developing the creative abilities needed to tackle wicked problems.

This is what it takes to prepare future-ready students, because one thing we know for sure about the decades to come is that they'll be filled with wicked problems.

Social planning experts Horst Rittel and Melvin Webber came up with the term "wicked problems" for challenges that are ridiculously difficult to address. They have three major traits:

—**Trait 1: Wicked problems are hard to identify.**
They're often buried as symptoms of other, more easily recognized issues. They can involve hundreds or thousands of factors. Some are contradictory, many are

constantly evolving, and nearly all of them are difficult to measure.

—Trait 2: Wicked problems cannot be solved through trial and error.
Either the stakes are too high and any error would be disastrous, or the solutions are moving targets that shift with every change.

—Trait 3: Wicked problems aren't self-contained.
Solving one element of a wicked problem can trigger the discovery—or creation—of even more problems.

The functional fixedness dilemma

So how do you tackle a wicked problem?

You teach students how to come up with wickedly unexpected solutions.

We do that by teaching them how to break patterns.

That's why it's such a tough challenge, especially for people who grew up learning formulas for problem-solving. The human brain is one giant pattern recognition machine. It's what allows us to learn from experience (including the experiences of others) and survive.

The pattern-based learning process starts early. As toddlers, we know that forks can be anything: hair combs, airplanes, tools for shaping mud piles, props for stuffed animals, musical instruments... But after a few thousand experiences, our growing brains recognize the "fork" pattern. After that, we stop using forks for anything but delivering food to our mouths.

This is good. When presented with a fork and a plate, we've incorporated an unconscious shortcut that frees our minds to focus on more complicated things, such as a conversation with a dining companion. Psychologists call these deeply ingrained, unconscious patterns "functional fixedness."

If we want to be successful adults, it's essential for us to be able to recognize and use such fixed patterns so we're not sidetracked all day by the infinite options around us.

But what happens when we're faced with an unrelated challenge, and a fork is the only tool at hand? We have to be able to toss the pattern aside to be able to see that a fork can also be used as a screwdriver, a wedge, or (apologies to Disney's *The Little Mermaid*) a dinglehopper. We're surrounded by tools that can have wide and varied functions, but we can only identify them if we can break out of seeing things in the functionally fixed patterns we're familiar with.

Dialing in

Consider breaking the pattern of a phone. Alexander Graham Bell patented the first telephone in 1876. Just 50 years later, the first "mobile phone" was invented: German military trains began communicating *in transit* using wireless telephone technology. Fast forward another 70 years: Bulky "car phones" started giving way to smaller, digital cellular phones. But these were still only telephones, allowing people to communicate by voice across long distances.

Who led the major functional fixedness break that allowed people to see portable telephones as mobile multi-tool devices?

Surprise: it wasn't Blackberry or Apple engineers. The break came in 1993, when the IBM Simon mobile phone was introduced. The Simon featured phone services, a pager, a FAX machine, email, and a PDA. It included a calendar, address book, clock, calculator, notepad, and touchscreen with QWERTY keyboard. The Simon even had predictive typing that would guess the next characters as you tapped with a stylus, and users could access "apps" by plugging in a memory card with a program.

All of these advances required both a thorough knowledge of the telephony industry—and practice in radical, pattern-breaking thinking.

Transforming the impossible

For a more historic example, consider a 20time project that began in 1896. A pair of bicycle repairmen from Dayton, Ohio began developing and testing theories of flight in their spare time. This was a massive undertaking in attacking functional fixedness, requiring them to first understand and then transform contemporary concepts of the physics of air flow, the construction of internal combustion engines, and the art of aircraft balance and control. Before they made some major leaps of intuition, early aircraft engineers around the world were held back by the assumption that movement in air would work in the same way as movement in water.

In December 1903, William and Orville Wright made the first controlled, sustained, powered aircraft flights in history on the windy beach at Kitty Hawk, North Carolina. But the announcement made barely a ripple—the general public knew plenty of gliders were being tested around the world at that time, and didn't understand the critical difference and extraordinary value of having a machine with truly controlled flight.

Fame (and steady funding) wouldn't arrive until the Wrights began giving world-changing demonstration flights at a racetrack in Le Mans, France—in August 1908, five years after their first success. Another decade would pass before people stopped reacting with shock on their first sight of an actual flying machine. Orville summed up the shift in functional fixedness in this message to a journalist in 1925:

"Human flight was generally looked upon as an impossibility, and ... scarcely anyone believed in it until he actually saw it with his own eyes."

Changing perceptions

Even when people *can* see with their own eyes, functional fixedness can cause major delays in solving wicked problems.

In the 1950s, a British epidemiologist at Oxford University noticed an alarming spike in the number of children developing fatal cancers. Using her skills as a medical researcher, Dr. Alice Stuart was able to identify the one demographic all of these children had in common: affluent parents.

Stuart dove deep into the data of these children's lives, sifting through thousands of environmental and experiential factors, until she found a common thread. Those most likely to develop cancers all came from fairly wealthy homes. That led to her discovery that, when these children were in utero, doctors had conducted prenatal X-rays to determine the fetuses' positions. The data showed that for children subjected to the scans, cancer rates doubled.

Stuart called for an immediate halt to the use of X-rays on pregnant women, but it took the medical establishment more than two decades to accept her data, duplicate it, and finally stop the practice.

Why? I blame functional fixedness.

During the first half of the 20th century, doctors enjoyed a position of incredible authority and public trust. Medical technology no less. If doctors on their own were seen as all-knowing, modern science seemed to make them infallible. Neither patients nor medical practitioners were prepared to break the pattern of seeing doctors as healers and accept the idea that they and their tools could cause harm.

Not until the 1970s did the medical establishment verify Stuart's work and stop administering X-rays to pregnant women. From that point on, Stuart's insights have helped save the lives of countless young people.

But in true wicked problem form, the solution triggered serious problems of its own.

The discovery of the dangers of X-rays contributed to a massive shift in public perception of the medical establishment. As a result, many of today's children fall victim to the exact opposite of the old pattern: intense suspicion of modern medicine, including an anti-vaccination movement that's triggered a resurgence of horrifying childhood diseases.

Solving wicked problems without see-sawing from one deadly crisis to another requires us to be open to non-intuitive approaches, even when they appear to contradict everything we believe we know.

Unfortunately, one of the core elements of modern education makes it incredibly difficult for students to practice exploring paradoxical views.

Where bribery fails

Many people think video games only teach violence, encourage laziness and rot the mind.

These people have not played good video games.

Video games are primarily computer-based learning programs. They teach the player a set of rules and skills, then reward the player for mastering those skills. Most video games are very difficult, and the brainpower required to get through them is enormous.

To teach my students about functional fixedness and how to break out of it, I show a beautifully designed 2010 puzzle platform video game called *Limbo*. The game's main character is a child attempting to travel through an extremely lethal jungle. Nearly every obstacle is fatal on the first encounter. But after being drowned, impaled, consumed by giant spiders, or falling to some other brutal end, the character reappears and gets another try.

It takes plenty of creative thinking to figure out how to get the child past each of the game's puzzles. I use this as the basis for an experiment, and split my students into two groups. I tell the first set: "Play this video game." I tell the second set: "If you solve the problem within 10 minutes, I'll pay you $50."

What we find is that the group who's told simply to play is able to solve a super-challenging puzzle much faster than the group I bribe. This flies in the face of everything we're taught about capitalism and competition. Having a cash incentive should encourage students to work faster and achieve more, but the opposite is true.

Why?

Tunnel vision.

Students who are offered a bribe get incredibly focused on outcomes. They want to win. They want the reward. The stress triggers their brains to drop into basic, supposedly reliable ways of viewing the tools around them.

We've already talked about how useful that kind of focus is, most of the time. When we have an already-solved problem to go after, all you have to do is follow the rules to get to the goal: kick the ball, memorize the text, follow the directions, use the tools...

With a novel problem, though, we don't know where we're going, let alone know how to get there. When we're also under pressure to achieve the unknown goal, every misstep feels like a disaster. We feel too stressed to create, let alone test, any strategies that violate known patterns.

Fortunately, the group of students who bring a sense of playfulness to their work tend to experience things differently. They're open to new and strange ideas that take them in unexpected, and thus successful, directions.

And so, after discovering that their character can't swim, can't survive in a pool long enough to walk across its bottom, can't use a nearby crate as a bridge, and can't use it for a raft—these "just playing" students will experiment with carrying the crate back one screen. There, they find a surprising way to use that traditional tool—one that gets them across the pool and on to the next challenge.

No pressure? No problem. A solution's just a few exploratory experiments away. *You can watch a video of this learning experience at 20time.org/limbo, and read more at 20time.org/fix.*

This isn't a fluke that only happens in my classroom. Many similar experiments conducted by professional researchers have shown that having an extrinsic motivator, such as a monetary bribe, fails to lead to innovative thinking. In fact, these studies show that extrinsic motivators actually *reduce* innovation.

To build or to destroy

Most Americans grow up in an environment that encourages functional fixedness, and that's a trend that's only worsening. Let's look at one of the great tools children once had for practicing creative, playful thinking, and how it's transforming into the complete opposite—toys that discourage creativity—today.

For decades, LEGO™ sets have challenged kids to use the bricks at hand to build anything they could imagine. Spaceships, castles, squirrels, time machines—everything was fair game. I remember building small cities with my friends, using not only LEGO bricks but toy dinosaurs, wooden blocks, flags made of toothpicks and paper towels, and model trains.

Today, the most popular LEGOs come in movie-themed packages. Follow the specific directions for where to place every single plastic brick, flag, and pre-painted figure, and you, too, can have your very own $150, 23-inch replica of a Star Wars™ Millennium Falcon! The problem is, not only do you have to follow the instructions to build it "right," but anyone exposed to pop culture can tell if you got it "wrong."

Now, I wouldn't complain if a miniature Millennium Falcon ended up on my desk at school, someday. These are cool toys that remind us of the wonders created on Hollywood screens. But I'd much prefer to set up my classroom as a safe place for kids to spend time designing their own versions of spacecraft and movie magic, using nothing but a random pile of plastic bricks and some leftover art supplies.

This isn't because I'm old fashioned. It's because I value young brains working out their own creative solutions, not following instruction guides for products already built by 10,000 other kids around the world.

When we offer children and teenagers tools for learning, we need to make sure they're delivered with an emphasis on permission to play. Rarely is there only one right way to use a LEGO, or a sheet of origami paper, or a pen. Instead, we're called to help young people understand the basics, then let them set their own goals and develop new paths for getting there.

Our classrooms can be refuges of creativity, giving students a safe place to experiment, meaningful reasons to do so, and celebrating the accidental discoveries along the way. Or they can be more examples of the licensed, prepackaged, no-surprises "play" experiences we so often give our kids today.

The importance of accidents

Why celebrate "accidental discoveries" and not just the intentional ones set up by our lesson plans?

Often, unplanned and unexpected experiences are what help us identify both a problem and its solution.

One great example comes from 3M, a corporation that produces more than 50,000 products worldwide. This company began providing a 15-percent time culture for its researchers in 1948. The approach paid off, leading to the creation of many new products and solutions.

Here's the story behind one of its most iconic.

In 1968, 3M's Dr. Spencer Silver was experimenting with adhesives, attempting to create something even stickier than super-glue. Instead, he accidentally developed something only slightly sticky. Silver was understandably disappointed, but came to believe there could be value in the pressure-sensitive adhesive he'd developed. But where?

Six years passed before that value appeared, and only as a result of another of 3M's creativity-positive policies: "permitted bootlegging." Art Fry, a 3M colleague, heard of Silver's creation and decided to test it on the back of the bookmark he used in his hymnbook. The paper stayed where he placed it, but he could easily move it to a new page to stick again, and again, and again. It didn't even leave a residue.

The Post-It® note was born.

This iconic product was the result of 3M giving its engineers the opportunities to collaborate and the freedom to play with problems, solutions and happy accidents, long before any end goals come into sight.

In the classroom, we can't wait six years for someone's ideas to reach their conclusion. What we can do is set aside protected time for students to practice trying, failing, improvising, trading ideas, and experiencing lots of happy accidents.

I suspect Silver and Fry would approve.

How to guide creative learners

Once you have a class engaged in open-minded, creative, playful experimenting, how do you get them through their happy accidents and to the point of actually solving wicked problems?

This is the part where we break out our Wise Old Sage voices and tell them:

—"Keep it simple."
Defining the problem may be the most difficult part of solving it. What's the simplest definable element they can reduce the problem to? Keep reducing until it's manageable with the time and resources available.

For instance, the problem of poverty includes the problem of hunger, which involves poor-quality food, which affects infant nutrition. The local WIC program could use funds to provide classes for infants and pregnant women.

That's a problem your student could achieve real results with.

—"Stay focused."

Don't let your students get distracted by the 100 waving tentacles of the monster they've taken on. Use clear, basic goals to keep them aiming at the heart of the beast.

—"Use the gifts you already have."

Resources don't always have to be tangible. Help students recognize the value of their personalities, their networks, and their world. Remind them to look for similar projects and draw on the experience and wisdom of earlier pioneers. Even the most innovative solutions are built on the failures and successes of those who have gone before.

—"Patience, my children."

Solving wicked problems takes time. It takes hundreds, even thousands of baby steps along the way. In today's fast-paced world of instant gratification, people of all ages need that reminder.

Show your students that the more experienced someone is at disrupting normal approaches, the more successful they're likely to be at solving wicked problems.

Praise actions, not talents

As your students progress, how will you celebrate and motivate them? Educators are learning that one of the most familiar tools we use can backfire if used poorly.

Many studies now show that children, especially girls, perform better when praised for their *actions* rather than their *traits*.

Imagine a classroom working on a series of difficult math problems. Students who are told "You're so smart," or "You're very gifted" when they solve a problem have a much harder time when things get more challenging. If they have to struggle on a math question, they come to believe it must mean that they're not intelligent or talented in math after all. So they give up.

Those praised for their persistence and careful attention, on the other hand, tend to try harder and longer on future questions. They know that their measure as a person isn't tied to their performance outcomes, but to their work along the way. As a result, they tend to do better down the road than those praised for their early promise. They keep on striving and creating.

Educators can help students understand that brainpower is not a fixed asset. Intelligence in any area is a skill that can be developed. Brainpower grows through effort and curiosity, failure and repetition.

It's an especially key point to emphasize with students taking on 20time. Truly creative, independent work should push them out of their comfort zones multiple times. Understanding this concept of value as a function of persistence can help students persist through the tough parts, practice their skills, and eventually produce meaningful, masterful results.

Catching tigers by the tail

Once a project is rolling, it's important to look up now and again and notice what effects it's having.

Especially the unexpected effects.

When solving wicked problems, the solutions we come up with for one area will end up affecting many other areas, as well. Good innovators anticipate this and look for ways to capitalize on those effects—without losing sight of their original goals, of course.

Remember how the IBM Simon transformed the perceived function of telephones? The engineers who first combined our needs for communication with calendars and calculators saw the potential for smartphones to do far, far more.

Steve Jobs and Apple had the vision to combine the power of a full computer with the portability of a mobile phone. In doing so, they transformed the world. Now, millions of people carry tools 24/7 that allow them to record, engage with, and explore their worlds with extraordinary ease and speed. With a few clicks and swipes, we have constant access to the newest and most transformative tools available.

And we can still make phone calls.

When we teach our 20time students to assess their progress and impact as they go, they are more able to adapt to the changes they're encountering and creating. They're able to learn faster from their failures, identify their successes, and see the potential for new successes down the road. Most important, they're better prepared to deal with the ever-transforming wicked problems they'll tackle someday.

Chapter II
How To Run A 20time Program

My first year of leading a class through 20time was a 20time project in itself. As we'll learn later in the book, that means I experienced a LOT of failure.

I'm looking forward to sharing those failures with you, because despite the bumps along the way, my class and I did achieve our first year goals: we made it through, we learned a ton, and through their projects, the students made a positive difference in their communities and the world.

I'm happy to say that, even after reading this book, anyone running their first 20time program is still going to make a ton of mistakes. (Yes, I'm happy about this—mistakes and failures are some of the best paths to innovation and learning.)

My hope is that by sharing my experiences, the mistakes *you* make will be a little more advanced and a lot more productive.

1: Communicating

Let's start with one of my first—and worst—failures: lack of communication.

When I first introduced The 20% Time Project, I did a terrible job letting people know about the program and why I was trusting teenagers to engage in self-led enterprise. I'd done a great deal of research exploring why this kind of project would help my students become better learners and problem solvers. I was convinced of its value.

So I launched it.

Without telling anybody.

Word got out that I was giving my students more freedom in their English class once a week. Thanks to the rumor mill, "more freedom" became "giving my students a free period each week." Can you guess what happened next?

Yep. I had an outraged father on my hands, furious that I was cheating his son out of learning time. Fortunately, once I explained exactly what I was doing, this irate dad became one of 20time's greatest supporters.

Now, I start out by sending parents a letter at the beginning of the year that outlines the entire project and the reasons behind it. *You can read a sample of the letter in the Appendices at the end of this book, or view and download a template at 20time.org/letter.*

What sort of responses does this letter get? So far, several parents have written back to thank me for giving their child this opportunity. Most don't respond at all, presumably because I answered all their questions.

Mission accomplished.

Earning buy-in

That's not the only communicating I do, of course.

With parents, I review the letter in person during our fall Back To School night and answer any questions they may have. Sometimes parents attend one of my talks where I show a video compilation of students describing their 20time projects—that's always an inspiring experience.

Throughout the year, I encourage parents to track what's happening by reading our classroom Twitter page. It's a fantastic way to communicate with both students and families, and it's the best way I've found to keep the whole process transparent.

Students themselves get to review the same letter outlining the project and the reasoning behind it at the start of the school year. This way, they know exactly what they're getting into and have a good sense of what a big deal it is. Then, during our weekly 20time sessions, we check in with each other to make sure they're staying on track and have the resources they need to move forward.

When it comes to communicating with administrators and colleagues, I'm lucky to be in a school that offers plenty of support. But I'm confident that my experience is not unique, and neither are those of dozens of other 20time educators. 20time is a framework most school communities are likely to encourage.

That said, before you dive in, I recommend letting your school's administrators know about the project. Describe your plan. Talk about how 20time projects offer terrific opportunities for meeting the standards of Common Core and our 21st century needs for collaboration, communication, critical thinking and creativity. You can also direct them to the extensive research documenting the rationale behind 20time and its effectiveness. *Check out the books and web resources listed in the Appendices and at 20time.org.*

The biggest concern I encounter from my colleagues is that students won't be motivated or passionate about the project. I tell them: Passion follows purpose. Just get them started. Once students understand that their project will help other people, they become incredibly motivated and excited to dive in.

When should I offer 20time?

There are as many different ways to structure 20time programs as there are teachers who implement them.

The first step is to reserve about 20 percent of students' in-class time to working on their projects. For many teachers, reserving one class period out of five is an obvious choice. Schools that use a block schedule might reserve a long period every two weeks.

I don't recommend using 20 percent of each class period. I've found that providing larger chunks of time leads to more productive work sessions than setting aside a few minutes a day.

I'm often asked if 20time projects have to take a full year. That depends on the class dynamic. I know of several teachers who offer 20time as a semester- or quarter-long project. That's great.

For me, I like having my students pursue a year-long project, because this provides more opportunities for both preparation and going deep. I also think there's value in long-term planning. Students need more experiences with it before we send them into the world.

It's important to know that students can't always use class time for their project. Many students take on challenges that require them to work at home, on sites off-campus, or with groups of people who are not in the class. I usually have these students focus their in-class sessions on writing their blog. Once that is finished, they can use the time for other school-related projects, with the expectation that they'll work on the 20time project on their own. These students must demonstrate to me through their blog that they're staying active and meeting their deliverables.

Finally, one of the biggest concerns I hear from teachers, administrators, parents and even students is: How can students complete all of their educational standards if they're also doing 20time?

I'll talk more about this in Part V: The Learning Game, but the short answer is: students will meet their content standards by doing 20time. Design your students' project requirements to meet the standards. For instance, when I taught English, I put a lot of emphasis on the writing components of the proposals, weekly blogs and presentations. Now that I teach technology, my classes focus on the online tools and components.

2: Getting the right idea

I love it when my students start out knowing exactly what they want to do. Some students hear me tell them that I want them to pursue independent projects for an authentic purpose, and they just nod and begin planning. (Most likely, these are former Montessori students.)

The reality, though, is that most of them have no idea what they want to do. Many students have never been asked, "What do you want to work on in class today?" These kids aren't thrilled when I introduce 20time.

"Hey, Mr. Teacher. You're the professional here. You're supposed to tell us what to do."

The first few years I piloted the project, I held a class brainstorm session to generate ideas for projects. I would ask students to go to the whiteboard with colored markers and get down as many ideas as they could. "There are no bad ideas," I told them.

They knew better.

Everyone who has ever been in school knows that one of the easiest ways to get labeled "dumb" is to come up with a bad idea, no matter how often the teacher says it's okay.

In 2010, I attended a workshop by Ewan McIntosh. He introduced me to the notion that seeking out bad solutions to complex problems often, paradoxically, yields the best solutions. As McIntosh explains on his blog:

> When you ask a room of professionals to come up with their "best" solutions to a problem, you tend to get great ideas, but not always the best ones. They can be contrived and almost always involve some self-censorship from the team: people don't offer anything up unless they feel, explicitly or subconsciously, that it will get buy-in from the rest of the team or committee. Ask people for their "worst" solutions to a problem and people tend not to hold back at all—laughs are had and the terrible ideas

flow. And while the initial suggestions might feel stupid, pointless or ridiculous to the originating team members, these awful ideas can take on a spectacular new lease on life in the hands of another, unrelated group.

McIntosh's findings suggest that there is a crucial difference between *allowing* bad ideas and *actively seeking* bad ideas—and that the latter approach is the best way to get ideas flowing. This led me to a new approach to brainstorming.

The Bad Idea Factory

After I introduce the concept of 20time, I call my students together and challenge them to generate as many awful ideas as possible.

And boy, can they generate bad ideas:

—"Create an invasive species and set it loose in the Monterey Bay Sanctuary."
—"Test people's reactions to flavor by slipping vinegar into their water."
—"Make a movie about grass growing."
—"See how many places we can plank in one year." (Google "planking" for an appreciation of how mind-bogglingly bad an idea this was.)

For more awesomely awful ideas, watch the "Bad Idea Factory 2013" video at 20time.org/bif.

Of course, the real purpose of The Bad Idea Factory isn't to come up with bad ideas. It's to expand students' view of what a project idea could be. And while I tell them to write as many bad ideas as they can, I also make it clear that if a good idea comes to mind, they should add it to the list.

I believe this exercise is so successful because it shuts off the critics in our brains. Who can be creative when something in our minds is constantly telling us that our ideas suck?

In addition, actively seeking bad ideas liberates students from functional fixedness. Instead of trying to fit their vision into an imaginary pattern for what a "20% Time Project" would look like, they break free of preconceptions and come up with ideas that are truly good and truly new.

What makes this process so much fun is seeing terrible ideas transform, after a little thinking, into awesome 20time projects. Here are two of my favorite examples:

—"I want to experience what it's like to be homeless for a week." (Will, 2012)
What a great Bad Idea! We decided that a high school student spending seven days and nights living on the streets was not safe enough to actually pull off, but we could certainly tweak the project into a Good Idea. Will spent the school year learning about issues around homelessness in our county, interviewing people without permanent homes, serving them, and spreading awareness.

—"I want to spend a month in a wheelchair." (Denny, 2013)
This one moved straight from the Bad Idea list to the Good Idea list. Denny did spend a month attending school in a wheelchair, gaining a great deal of insight into how our campus could be more accessible to people with disabilities. The old, rutted dirt path that led to his Latin class was particularly tough. Now, York School boasts a lovely concrete walkway that makes all its classrooms accessible.

Perhaps the best thing about The Bad Idea Project is the tone it sets for the class at the beginning of the year. It proves to students that the classroom is going to be one where play and creativity are held in high regard, where students are free to express risky thoughts, and where having fun is better than trying to be perfect. *You can find a quick guide to running a Bad Idea Factory in the Appendices.*

Moon Shot Thinking

What is "Moon Shot Thinking"?

Made famous by Google CEO Larry Page (a Montessori alum), moon shots inspire us to stop tweaking existing solutions and solve problems by going big, instead. Really big. They encourage us to rethink the problem entirely, aim incredibly high.

The goal is to change our pattern from seeking 10 percent improvements to pushing for 10 times beyond the norm.

In other words, shoot for the moon.

This thought tool is critical for dealing with our world's most important wicked problems. We've got serious issues to tackle, ranging from environmental disasters like climate change and polluted water to man-made crises like global terrorism and lack of education.

These major problems are not solved by making the status quo just a little bit better. It needs to be made dramatically better, if not completely reversed. That's because the planet needs completely disruptive solutions. We can't get there without breaking the habit of using conventional approaches.

It starts with looking at examples of recent moon shot thinking that have already transformed the 21st century.

—Project Loon

Access to the Internet has become a human right—as important as running water and electricity to the survival and advancement of communities. But while a single pipeline can provide broadband Internet to millions of customers in a city, rural Internet doesn't scale as well.

Farmers in remote areas without Internet don't have access to the weather data and market information that others do. That makes it much more difficult to grow and sell the crops that support their families. The same applies to business leaders, politicians, medical workers, educators and families in rural areas worldwide. But pipelines and satellites have proven far too expensive to address the need.

How to solve the rural Internet roadblocks?

A breakthrough came when Google X (the company's laboratory dedicated to moon shots) dove into the project. Using technology from the 1800s, they rigged balloons with radio transmitters that can distribute free Internet access reliably—and affordably—from the air.

The balloons are flown at about 70,000 feet above the earth. They're propelled by predictable wind currents, powered by solar cells, and controlled with a fan that balances their helium and air chambers. Each balloon carries a 3G transceiver providing Internet broadband access to rural communities.

If you're looking for an inspirational video break, check out Google's promotion of this project at 20time.org/loon. I've watched this video and shown it to groups well over 50 times, and it still makes me tear up a little when she says: "That's why we're giving it a try."

—The Innovation Lab

Not every moon shot is about changing the world. Sometimes, it just makes it a better place to live.

Lowe's, the home improvement retailer, created its Innovation Lab in 2013 to tackle two big challenges: online-only shopping and consumer retention.

This wasn't your usual laboratory of hard-core scientists and engineers, though. Lowe's brought in science fiction writers to help the teams come up with the big ideas that would move the brand forward.

After feeding the writers all of their market research and data on the customer experience Lowe's strives to create, the writers drafted stories about potential customers to help the company envision a more ideal future.

The first project to emerge? Giving uncertain homeowners the chance to do some envisioning of their own.

The lab created a 20-foot by 20-foot holographic projection chamber for customers who come to the actual brick-and-mortar store. After using an iPad app to design their project, drawing on the built-in images of nearly every item in the Lowe's warehouse, they can step into the middle of their design and walk around, seeing how it looks and feels.

Whatever's next for Lowe's, you can bet on it being innovative.

—The Google Self-driving Car

Here's a problem: More than 1 billion automobiles exist today, shaping cities and livelihoods the world over. But they come at a terrible cost.

About 1.3 million people die each year in vehicle crashes. In the United States alone, about 35,000 lives are lost. And almost every crash is the result of human factors, from driver error to reaction speed.

The solutions so far have been safe driving campaigns, better-designed vehicles and roadways, and luck. Some engineers at Google X decided those solutions weren't good enough. With the help of car-mounted lasers, radar, proximity sensors, extremely detailed maps and remote computer farms, their self-driving vehicles have logged 700,000 autonomous miles as of spring 2014—and only two crashes, apparently occurring only when a human passenger was actively operating the vehicle.

The moon shot of creating a transportation system of self-guided, accident-preventing vehicles just may save thousands of lives worldwide each day.

That's a moon shot worth encouraging.

Land among the stars

So what do moon shots look like in the classroom? Something like the adage: "Shoot for the moon. Even if you miss, you'll land among the stars."

My first encounter with a real moon shot came the first time I suggested a 20time project, in the fall of 2009.

One of my senior English students, Robin Clark, came up with the idea of holding a low-tech art show for young people in Monterey and Santa Cruz counties. She proposed sending postcards to teachers, asking their students to send in pieces of art for display.

The twist? They were told to ship them by post without any packaging, actually putting stamps and addresses directly on each piece.

"That's a super cool idea," I told her, "but I think you're going to put in a lot of effort, and no one will send you any artwork. Is there any way we can scale this back a little bit, maybe keep it just to York students?"

Robin—who was both an artist heavily involved in a local youth arts community and a black belt in jujutsu—said no.

"I really want teachers at other schools," she said.

And said again. And again. Until, after several weeks of my attempts to convince her to change her project, I finally gave the okay.

February rolled around, when Robin expected the first art pieces to arrive. She got nothing. March rolled around, and she got nothing. April rolled around, and she got nothing.

I started feeling really badly for her. I was disappointed, too. (Although I admit to having some not-so-grown-up thoughts: "I told you so! You should have listened to me.")

Finally, in early May, a few pieces showed up in the mail. The next day, there were more. Then more. By the end of May, Robin was overwhelmed by hundreds of art submissions.

She was able to pack a local coffee shop with amazing student art from throughout the region. Local artists of all ages came to the official opening event, our region's newspapers were on scene, and Robin went on to publish a book based on the show.

Her project was an unbelievable success. Robin later told me it was the most meaningful experience of her year.

I learned a ton from the students who took part in 20time that year. But the biggest lesson I learned was to never, ever discourage someone for thinking too big.

Now, I want students to think as big as they can. If they say they want their video to get a million views, I say "Go for it." You never know when someone with enough energy will pull something incredible off.

We need to create environments where students get to practice moon shots, so they're ready to take on the really big problems that adults have not been able to solve so far. That's because the solutions to those problems are not obvious. They're going to be totally surprising. Unless our kids are comfortable thinking way, way outside the box, they're going to get stuck in the same kind of thinking that helped create and perpetuate the problems in the first place.

So when it's time for students to come up with a 20time project idea, give them permission to think big. Let them play in the Bad Idea Factory for awhile and come up with really horrible, off-the-wall solutions.

There's a good chance they'll start up a path no one else has attempted and find exactly what the world needs, just beyond the sign that reads: "Impossible."

Don't crash and burn

Of course, not every moon shot will even make it out of the atmosphere. What happens when a project collapses halfway through the year?

We pivot.

As teachers, one of our main responsibilities in leading a 20time project is helping students stay on track. That includes knowing when it's time to abandon ship.

When a project just isn't coming together as planned, help your students to recognize what's happening, then use what they've learned so far to adjust the project or come up with a new one.

Celebrate those failures, frame them as learning opportunities, and above all, keep moving forward. That may be the most important lesson any of your students can learn from 20time.

3: Going It Alone? Not On 20time

Whenever I introduce a new class project, I get two questions: "Can we work in groups?" and "Do we have to work in groups?"

That's humanity, right? Some of us derive energy from working with other people. Others find greater motivation in solitude.

If what we do in our classrooms is about preparing our students for adulthood, we need to provide opportunities for both individual and group activities. Students deserve a chance to shine on their own. They also desperately need safe opportunities to develop the communication and social skills they'll need to navigate team projects in the future. After all, most creative pursuits that result in real-world solutions involve teamwork.

But if we compare "school culture" with "career culture," it's easy to see that schools place a premium on solo work. Not only do we teachers often set up our classroom experiences on the solo model, our best students are all too willing to keep it that way. Many learned early on that the student who is most concerned with his or her grade ends up doing all of the group's work. The only thing these kids expect to learn from a group project is what it feels like to get stabbed in the back.

Projects like ours are an opportunity to create a balance. I know some teachers who actually require that students work in teams on projects like these. I've come very close to doing so myself. However, each year I get students who really want to take this opportunity to focus on their own work, and I've seen enough successful solo projects to continue to approve them.

When I allow students to take on a project by themselves, however, they still get the chance to practice collaboration. In my classroom, 20time projects must be created to serve an external audience—not just a personal, pet passion. The students can only come to understand that audience by connecting with its members throughout the project, conducting interviews and getting feedback along the way.

The students also work with mentors and organizations to help make their projects a success. Finally, their classmates will be the ones helping them practice and refine their final presentations.

For example, I allowed Maddie to conduct a solo 20time project during the 2013-2014 school year. Her goal was to encourage people to visit secondhand shops and buy clothes and other items there instead of at major brand stores. She wanted to help her community and peers reduce conspicuous consumption, reuse resources, fight destructive definitions of beauty, and support the work many thrift organizations do in their communities. Throughout the year, Maddie worked very closely with Goodwill staff and fellow teenagers to collect donations and spread the message. Even though her 20time was a solo project, she hardly ever worked alone.

A few tips on groups

For those who choose to work in groups, I've found the following structures help keep engagement balanced.

1. Keep groups to no more than four students.

Groups of five or more seem to have a harder time staying focused and distributing tasks equally among the participants. It's also harder for me to make sure they're all on track.

2. Students must blog.

I require that each individual working on a 20time project submit a unique weekly blog post, so I know what each student is doing. More on these blogs later.

3. Use check-in conversations.

Nothing beats a good, old-fashioned conversation. It's good to check in with students, both as a class and one-on-one, and ask questions about how the group work is going, what challenges are coming up, and how they're negotiating them. They also give students a chance to practice dealing with group work dramas before their careers are on the line.

4. Use technology to improve group work.

Classrooms have very close to universal access to unlimited creation tools that didn't exist 10 to 20 years ago.

Here's a short list of the free technologies you can use to help groups communicate, coordinate, track participation and inspire their communities: Google Docs, Google Forms, Blogger, YouTube, Twitter, Facebook. *Find out more about using these as classroom tools at 20time.org.*

Some students have less access to online and computer tools than others due to home situations or other issues. They will be at a disadvantage, but it's not a reason for classes to not use technology at all.

Instead, I encourage you to put your classroom's energy into making the most of what's available and working to ensure every student has the technology knowledge and access they need to succeed.

Unmotivated students

What's the core issue when students in a group aren't pulling their weight? It's almost always a lack of motivation.

I doubt there's ever been a classroom where every student has turned in all of their work beautifully, enthusiastically and with complete motivation. In fact, I'd say a majority of students will actively shut down and fail to participate when you first give an assignment.

20time is no exception. Some students will resist out of fear, confusion and overwhelm. Some will be crippled by self-doubt and perfectionism. Some are caught up in a power struggle with authority, and you and the project are caught in the cross-fire. Some are battling a blend of all three!

Obviously, each of these students will need a different approach to help them along. For the anxious students, a little extra guidance and support on venturing into independent work can go a long way.

For those who can't work up a scrap of an idea for a project, I ask what they're passionate about. What are they excited about doing after school? On the weekends? Over the summer? Then we brainstorm ways to turn some element of their passion into a 20time project.

When students tell me they're not passionate about anything, it feels tragic. But I can't force them to get excited. Instead, I think it's totally appropriate to assign such students a service project. If they can't (or won't) come up with a charity or organization that needs volunteers, I find one for them. I say: "Your job is to go work for this organization, document your work using photos and videos, and come back to share your experience. I don't care if you're passionate about it. All I care about is that you help somebody."

Passion stems from that experience, every time. I've never met a single human being who doesn't get passionate about helping other people. No matter how hard they fight it, even the most unmotivated students will get meaning out of that process.

Of course, even students who create amazing projects can frustrate the heck out of a teacher. There's always a percentage who, regardless of how incredible their product is and how many reminders they receive, don't do some part of the algorithmic work—their proposal, their blog, their elevator speech, their presentation. That's their responsibility. In those cases, I grade them accordingly. For instance, late blog entries don't get credit.

What's refreshing about 20time is that students who are usually unmotivated get absolutely fired up on this assignment. They perform amazingly well and produce remarkable, astounding academic work—because they get to be immersed in something they chose and they care about.

Working in a small group can be part of that motivation. One of my students (we'll call him Linus) was notorious for freezing up when asked to submit writing assignments or presentations. The blank screen was just too overwhelming. Whenever Linus did create something, he was so dissatisfied, he refused to turn it in.

I pleaded with him over and over, pointing out that an average or below-average grade on any assignment would be enormously better than a zero. That logic rarely worked.

For his 20time, Linus paired up with a high-performing student. I worried that Linus wouldn't contribute enough to the project, and his partner would be left on the hook.

During rehearsal for the final presentations, I was disappointed (but not surprised) that Linus wasn't prepared. We talked about how important it was for him to have something to present, but I wasn't getting a reaction…until I told him that his partner was depending on him to do this. Something finally seemed to click. By presentation day, Linus had fully delivered on his obligation to present his work, and he did an amazing job.

The crowd went wild.

4: The Proposal

Great ideas are everywhere—for books, gadgets, movies, businesses.

What matters is execution.

Once students know what they'd like to do for 20time, they must convince their classmates and convince me—but they can't do that without creating the structures to make their vision real.

That's what a formal proposal helps them do. It's not just a tool for measuring the viability of a project—or getting a grade. It's about setting up students for success by showing them how to plan for and navigate major challenges along the way.

I give them a template to follow, helping make sure they include all the elements of a successful proposal:

—Team members' names
—Project title and summary

—Problem that needs to be solved
—Who it will benefit
—Estimated timeline of deliverables and deadlines
—The intended result, physical or digital
—Equipment and costs required
—Inspiring conclusion

View a sample template in the Appendices of this book, or download a formatted version at 20time.org/proposal.

The proposal is one of the major writing assignments I require as a part of 20time projects, and I grade them on both style and substance.

Do I help students with their proposals? Absolutely. This is not an assignment designed to test existing knowledge. It's about fostering skills, translating pie-in-the-sky ideas into real-life projects, and ensuring that students have a roadmap for success.

I don't write the proposals for them, but I often nudge students to get more specific about their details. For example, how will a team seeking international pen pals identify fellow teens to write to? How will they interest those teens enough to write back? How will they measure the erosion of cultural and language barriers during the project?

Regarding resources, it's important to help students gain experience around working with money and connections. Help them get creative about their funding. Instead of just asking their families to pay their project costs, they could develop partnerships and work out trades with related businesses, take on a related job to help bring in cash, seek donations of goods and materials from the community, or set up a crowdfunding campaign.

(This book was funded in just such a way. Check out the crowdfunding page at kickstarter.com/projects/brookhouser/the-20time-project.)

I also encourage students to overestimate how long it will take them to manage each element by as much as three times their original guess. For example, I suggested that the pen pal team start drafting profiles at least two months earlier than they'd planned, and that they print and assemble their journal of letters throughout the year to avoid an overwhelming rush at the end.

Finally, I play devil's advocate, challenging students to prepare for obstacles and quandaries along the way. What will the letter writers do if their pen pals don't respond? What if Abdul and Surya write once, but never again? What if the pen pals ask for money to help their families and communities? What if they want to arrange a visit? Help them build success in advance.

5: Mentors Are Rare And Precious

"Mr. Brookhouser, we want to build a foundry for our 20time project."

I couldn't really remember what a foundry was, but I knew it had something to do with melting metal.

"That sounds dangerous...and fun. What do you know about building a foundry?"

"Nothing."

"Same here. Let's get help from someone who does."

Thus, the mentor program was born.

This conversation happened in 2012, several years after I began offering 20time. Many students were taking on projects about which I had very little or no expertise, and I knew their work would be more successful with expert adult guidance.

The problem was, I didn't know how to implement a mentor program. That first year, the program basically failed.

I decided that each student would write a formal letter of introduction asking for support from an adult they and their parents trusted. Getting parents involved was a good idea. So was writing a formal letter.

Things started falling apart when I mandated that each student contact their mentor at least once a month to seek guidance.

From the failures that followed, I learned:

—Adults are busy, and asking students to depend on them for guidance can set both up for failure.

—Students need coaching on how to solicit support from professional adults, or adults can be left confused about what is expected of them.

—Teachers need a system to track student-mentor relationships and make sure they're working on both sides.

Fortunately, a few of these mentoring relationships somehow managed to flourish. My metal-minded students found a great guide in building their foundry, who helped them successfully melt aluminum into a mold. (I later learned this is no trivial task!) Another group of students, who wanted to learn to build an eco-friendly dream house, connected with a local architect. He guided these students through complex software and the thousands of design elements involved in creating the houses we live in and pass each day.

Setting the stage for building mutually beneficial relationships between students and professionals is an important benefit of 20time. But if you decide to offer this opportunity, I recommend flexibility.

Rather than requiring monthly check-ins, I have my students contact a professional and ask for two points of contact during the school year. After the initial inquiry, the first contact should come when the project is starting to gear up. The students then update the professional about the project's status and request feedback and suggestions.

If a relationship develops where the student and adult work closely throughout the year, great. But I encourage you to let that happen naturally. In many cases, the mentor will offer little to no feedback, and the student should be free to wait until the project is completed to seek additional comments or suggestions.

6: The Blog

Writing plays a major role in 20time. This is not just because I've been an English teacher. It's because no matter how amazing a project is, good verbal and written communication are critical to helping people understand and support it. Even Google engineers have to write progress reports once in awhile.

I've found that one of the best tools for helping 20time students stay on track is the blog. I require that all students submit a post each week of no fewer than 150 words, charting the progress of their projects. Each blog post must contain an image that the blogger has the right to publish. Each post must address the past, present, and future of the project.

If more than one person is working on the same project, each student must make an individual weekly post.

These requirements help students be more thoughtful about their projects, taking stock of the successes and shortcomings so far. The blog also becomes concrete evidence of the effort needed to produce the project. This provides a lively visual record that helps me understand how each group's work is evolving while holding students accountable to their goals.

So what do these blogs look like?

First, students discuss what has happened during the past week. What have they accomplished? What has gone wrong? What challenges have they faced? What have they learned through the process? More importantly, how have their skills improved over the past week? This last question helps students recognize and demonstrate mastery, a key motivator.

I also ask them to assess their overall progress. Are they on track for an on-time delivery? What adjustments need to be made to the timeline?

As I read the blogs, I make judgment calls on whether it's time to step in and guide students in making appropriate changes. Some will be just fine adjusting on their own or finding ways to renew their motivation. If I see a group spinning its wheels and getting frustrated or bored, I intervene.

The single most effective thing I've found to do in these situations is to bring the students' focus back to their audience.

Finally, the blog is a place to write about what's next. Since we adopt a bias for action in my classrooms, I require my students to document their next actions in advance. I'm talking about actions that require hands manipulating atoms (even if they're atoms on a keyboard). I don't want students to write, "My next action will be to figure out how to procrastinate less."

The way to procrastinate less is to focus on a next action. I'd rather see: "My next action is to sketch five drawings of how the concert stage should be arranged," or "My next action is to write 2,000 more words of my novel, whether I like the result or not," or "My next action is to find three people who might be users of my software, deliver my elevator pitch to them, and ask for feedback."

When it comes to format, as long as students have written responses to the three core questions that I can easily access online, then the host they use doesn't matter. They could use Blogger, Reddit, Tumblr, Wordpress. Or they could not use a blogging platform at all. Traditional blogs are great for longer-form writing, but students have many other tools for documenting projects.

- **Instagram / Flickr / Pinterest:** Simple photo sharing—ideally with captions.
- **YouTube / Vimeo:** Students can show themselves and their work through a video blog.
- **SoundCloud:** Like YouTube, but just sound. Great for podcasters and musicians.
- **Twitter:** Perfect for brief, non-intimidating updates of 140 characters or fewer.
- **Facebook / Google+:** Facebook has the user base. Google+ has the interactive tools.

Whatever the format, the blogs are required to be some form of a nonfiction narrative that lets me know exactly what students are doing so I can keep them accountable. There's some room for creativity, but if a group gets too far out into poetry and artistic expressions, I reel them back in.

Let the creativity come out in the 20time project itself.

A note for classroom instructors: Reading dozens and dozens of blogs is initially inspiring. Then it becomes tedious. Even with RSS aggregators, there are simply too many websites to visit. It takes too much time to track all the posts.

I credit my friend Alice Chen, who leads 20time projects in her southern California classroom, for a terrific solution.

Alice creates a Google Form and shares it with her students. Each time a submission is due, they log on, paste an actual copy of the blog in a text field, and include a link to the blog itself. With this form, she can read all of her students' creations in one scan of a spreadsheet and see exactly when they were posted.

Brilliant!

Check out the form at 20time.org/blogcheck.

Google's Blogger

One of the easiest tools for setting up and managing a student blog is Blogger, which is built into every Google account. Here's how to use it:

1. Go to google.com.
2. Log in or create an account.
3. Click the Apps icon at the top of the screen (it looks like a box of small squares). Scroll down to the Blogger link and click it.
4. You'll be taken to your Blogger Dashboard. Click the "New blog" button and follow the instructions on the screen.
5. Adjust the blog's visibility settings to control who can view the posts, limiting them to just classmates, schoolmates or the local community, or opening them to the entire world.

That's it!

The power of the image

Effective blogs use images.

Reading a long block of text is fine for a book or even a Kindle, but online is another matter. The Internet is a visual medium, where we've come to expect imagery.

It's not just the cultural agreement that's grown up around Internet usage. Many of us are visual thinkers who remember pictures better than we do the content or message. What a great way to connect with an audience!

I require students to use images on their blogs because it forces them to think of their 20time projects in a visual way and use multiple intelligences to convey information about their progress. Plus, it makes for a terrifically engaging visual record.

So what does the image requirement involve?

The simplest, most interesting and most relevant way students meet this requirement is to take their own photos of their work (and/or team) and upload it to the blog. I tell students that once they snap a photo, whether it's with a cell phone or a $1,000 camera, they are instantly granted copyright privileges on that creative work. No one is permitted to copy or publish that image without their permission, and they don't even need to file it with the U.S. Copyright Office. This knowledge often sparks more pride of ownership and motivates students to take better images.

What if students want to use an image they didn't create? I tell them that if they know or can connect with the owner, they can request written permission to use the creator's work. Otherwise, they can only use images that are clearly in the public domain or have been licensed through Creative Commons.

Public domain

U.S. copyright law is highly complex, but in general, if the creator of a work has been dead for 100 years or more, their work can be reused without violating law. Students can do whatever they want with the 500-year-old image of the *Mona Lisa*, but Picasso's *Guernica* is protected until 2037.

Photos taken by the U.S. government are almost always in the public domain and may be used, published, and remixed without any attribution. We taxpayers paid for those images, so we're allowed to use them. (Flickr provides a good way to find U.S. government images at flickr.com/search/?w=usg.)

Wikipedia is another great resource for images. Nearly all images posted on Wikipedia pages are available for reuse.

Your best source may be the related site Wikimedia, which offers more than 20 million free-to-use media files from its site at commons.wikimedia.org, as well as comprehensive lists of international online archives featuring public imagery.

Creative Commons

Many writers, photographers, and other artists have found value in relinquishing their copyright and letting the public publish their work through the Creative Commons license (creativecommons.org).

One of my favorite musicians, Jonathan Coulton, has licensed his work this way. His fans are welcome to share his music freely, make videos based on his music, and even remix his work. Coulton only asks that he be properly named as the original source and that these new productions be non-commercial.

What does he get out of the deal? Exposure. While Coulton's not a rock star, he has a very strong following on the Internet, his shows are frequently sold out, and he can make a comfortable living making music by giving it away.

Students can find images with a Creative Commons license using Google Advanced Image Search page. The usage rights filter currently lives at the bottom of this page. Select "free to use or share," and begin searching. Most of these images require attribution, so when I find an image I like, I dig into its source and look for an owner to give proper credit.

Should the blog be public?

Blogging is almost always more fun with readers and commenters. When students see comments on their blog, they get a surge of endorphins, which is always a good motivator. They're also likely to feel a sense of recognition, value, and purpose.

On the other hand, many families and educators are concerned about online privacy and safety. There are many ways of addressing this, from educating students about the risks and ways to protect themselves to using technology to control who sees what on a page. For instance, Blogger settings let users prevent their blogs from being publicly listed by search engines. This ensures security through obscurity — and also ensures no comments. Which is why I recommend that as students get older, they increase the reach of the blog.

At the least, class members should be encouraged to read and comment on each other's blogs. (That may even become one of the requirements for your class's 20time projects.)

Students can also find blogging partners at quadblogging.net or through a Twitter #20time hashtag, where they can connect with students engaging in project-based learning around the world. The site kidblog.org provides a more private venue for students to try out blogging under teacher guidance.

The truth is, the Internet is an excellent tool for helping like-minded teachers and students find each other. One of the pitfalls of being a teacher is that it's kind of lonely when it's just you and the kids in your classroom. And one of the pitfalls of classrooms is they don't expose us to the diverse world beyond their walls. That's why more and more educators are promoting "Personal Learning Communities," where we can search for students and educators working on similar projects. Once those connections are made, we can learn from people with different experiences and new perspectives. Sharing our ideas provides motivation, inspiration, and many more opportunities to grow.

7: The Elevator Pitch

One of the elements of my mid-year exam is the 20time Elevator Pitch. The term comes from the notion that innovators with a great idea might find themselves in an elevator with a powerful investor. They'll have a very short period of time to convince this investor to buy into their idea, and need to make their case as succinctly and persuasively as possible.

For this assignment, I ask my students to prepare and memorize a 30-second pitch about their 20time project. I tell them that good elevator pitches have two parts: they establish a problem and explain how to solve it. Elevator pitches should also be catchy, easy to understand, convincing, and inspiring.

I tell my students to deliver their pitch in a way that compels me to pull out my wallet and write a check to support their work. (I leave my checkbook at home that day just in case some do.)

The outline for a good elevator pitch:

1. Problem statement
Explain what is wrong with the status quo, and why it's a significant problem.
2. It gets worse
Explain how failing to solve this problem could cause more problems.
3. Glimmer of hope
Suggest that the situation is not irreversible.
4. The novel solution
Explain how a new idea can help solve the problem.
5. The credible authority
Demonstrate that you are the right person to solve it.
6. The vision
Inspire the audience by painting a picture of how the world looks better with this problem solved.

Here's an example of how to help students create a winning elevator pitch.

Student Draft 1

For my 20time project, I want to create a phone app that helps me know what class I have next. I have always loved computers and programming and I believe that creating an app will help me learn more about app design. I am so excited about this project and I hope you are as well.

Teacher Feedback

This is a decent start, but it needs work to be more compelling to the audience. Your parents, grandparents, and even teachers care about what you love and how excited you are about learning. The strangers you meet on the elevator don't care at all. They have their own families to care about. Rather than talking about how great the project is for you, talk about how great it is for others — the people it will serve.

The language is also fairly boring. Start by painting a picture of the problem. In film, most scenes begin with an establishing shot of the wider environment. What kind of picture can you create with the first sentence that will catch people's interest and make them want to know more?

Student Draft 2

Millions of students around the world have class schedules that change on a daily basis, causing confusion, anxiety and (worse!) tardiness. Minutes of missed class time multiply to hours, which multiply to days and eventually years of missed learning opportunities, simply because students don't know where their next class is.

What if your phone told you the location of your next class? What if it told you how long you had to get there? What if it calculated how long it would take you to get from where you are now, to your locker, to your class...even with a bathroom break?

As a highly experienced software developer, I can make this app a reality and help students concentrate their brain power on thinking about class, not class schedules.

Teacher Feedback
I can't wait to see your project and use it myself!

For more examples of great elevator pitches, check out the videos at 20time.org/elevator.

8: The Best 5 Minutes Of Your Life

If you study anthropological history, you'll notice something that most cultures throughout history have treasured—but is missing from our own.

It's pageantry. Rites of passage. The elevation of a simple happening into a formal, ritual celebration signifying transformation and growth.

I very much want to create a signature event in the lives of my students to help them truly internalize what they've accomplished. So I strive to make the final presentation of their work as big a deal as possible—a true pageant of ideas and accomplishments.

Instead of a final exam, I have my students present their 20time projects in the style of a TED Talk. The annual TED (Technology, Entertainment, Design) Conference is one of the most vibrant, popular and successful lecture series ever created. It's especially relevant for my students, since the annual conference got its start in 1990 right here in Monterey. TED invites speakers from all walks of life to present their best ideas in the most innovative, engaging ways they can.

My students are a couple of decades younger than the average TED speaker; our production budget is a couple of degrees of magnitude smaller. But their ideas are just as diverse and inspiring. With the right coaching and setup, the performances offered on our school stage create a truly uplifting community celebration recognizing the impact of their work.

Here's how we do it.

1. Find the motivation

I ask my students to give me the best five minutes of their lives. Their job is to inspire me and the rest of the audience — their peers, families, school staff and friends, community members and journalists — with the story of their 20time experience.

I tell them that this presentation will be the culmination of a full year of creative effort, and their best chance to show off their projects. It's like a senior project or a college thesis. They can bring in their physical creations, give live demonstrations, or show images and short videos of their experiences for all to see.

My students must use their talks to demonstrate what inspired them to solve their particular problem in their own unique ways. They're asked to address all of the challenges they faced over the course of the year, followed by an inspiring conclusion.

No pressure, right?

It sounds intimidating, but I've found that when students understand the magnitude of a challenge and the personal meaning behind it, they rise to that challenge. They give more than they otherwise would: more time, more energy, more effort, more enthusiasm. It doesn't hurt that in this case, the project is a legitimate chance to brag about how awesome they and their work really are.

That said, stage fright is a real and debilitating challenge. The skill of public speaking is like a superpower, and very, very few people have it. In fact, most people fear public speaking more than death. For teenagers, whose lives often revolve around impressing others, the fear can be even worse. But it's worth pushing our young people through the fear. No matter what direction they take their lives, whether it's in business or politics or relationships or community building, if they know how to speak in front of a large group, they will become more powerful. (I only hope they use that power for good!)

The key is in helping students realize that when they feel nerves, it's a good thing. I tell my students: "If you're afraid while you're up on that stage, it means you're a human being with a pulse."

It also means that what they're doing matters to them. Their bodies are saying: "It's time to perform! Here's the energy you need to do it." So teach teens to say "I'm so excited" instead of "I'm so nervous." This lets them channel their energy into inspiring their audience—instead of running off the stage.

Help your students learn that our human minds can convince us of anything. Our thoughts can make us fail or make us succeed. Like Olympic athletes before they compete, have your students close their eyes and visualize delivering the perfect performance. Let them visualize being challenged and being successful.

Then—let them perform.

2. Learn the model

The better the model, the better the performance. Before preparing their 20time presentations, I show my classroom some of the best TED talks online, getting students familiar with the style and quality of presentation being asked of them. We critique these pro-level talks. What worked? What moments were memorable and inspiring? What didn't capture attention or feel as true?

We start by watching the following two TED talks: Ron Finley's "A Guerilla Gardener In South Central L.A.," and musician Amanda Palmer's "The Art of Asking."

(Finley, you'll notice, uses a few colorful words, so be sure to watch it before deciding to show his talk to students. In my classroom, we use it as a launchpad to discuss how people earn the right to use "inappropriate" language.)

Both talks cover what could be 20time projects. Finley created an audience by planting gardens in his run-down neighborhood's abandoned lots and curbside lawns, then sharing the food with hungry neighbors. Palmer trusted her audience to help her band find places to stay and to perform, and eventually to stop charging for her work. Like any other 20time experience, these were experiments in connecting with an audience and helping those people through creativity and effort.

Finley and Palmer also give unbelievable performances. Their talks are delivered with passion, humor, character and strong engagement with the audience, all things I encourage my students to deliver, as well. I point out the many ways humor can make a talk memorable: identifying paradoxes, pointing out follies, creating situational irony, using timing and contrast to surprise and delight.

Finally, these talks are terrific examples of how to use slides. Using images ranging from abandoned lots to the 8-Foot Bride, Finley and Palmer illustrated what they were speaking about in ways that enhanced rather than distracted from their messages. *Check the videos out at 20time.org/TED.*

Most TED talks end at 18 minutes. How long should your students' talks last? The short answer is: whatever length works best for your class. If you're homeschooling three kids, they could each spend a full day demonstrating their work and its impact on the community. If you're running five classes of 40 students each (my sympathies), you might keep them to one or two minutes each.

Or you could hold a contest. All students must deliver their presentation to their class, but only the very best presentations, as voted on by you and their peers, get to be shared in a community event.

My student groups must give presentations that run between four and five minutes. I've found that to be the sweet spot for my teens—long enough for them to go beyond the dry facts and share the emotional impact of their projects, but short enough to keep the work manageable and the audience interested. This works out to about 10 presentations an hour, including transitions.

We rehearse the timing until we're sure the presentations won't run late or wrap up too quickly. This is a community event, and needs to honor guests' time commitments (and attention spans) while providing both entertainment and value.

3. Avoid slideshow hell

We then talk about the curse of almost every educational training session, boardroom meeting and formal lecture, ever: slideshows.

Slides, all too often, are boring, irrelevant, overcrowded and worse—distracting. I spend a lot of time talking with my classes about "slideshow hell": people who read bullet points aloud to the audience, slides packed with fancy design themes and frames, weird transitions involving cartwheeling cartoon characters and dizzying animations, and so on.

Why use slides at all? Because the idea is to create a memorable talk, and memories are much stronger when reinforced by images and not words.

For their presentations, my students follow the TED model, using their slides to share images that illustrate what they accomplished with their project. At TED, most slides feature images alone. They dominate the entire screen—no frame. If any text is used, it's very brief and does no more than reinforce what the speaker is saying to the audience.

Anyone who uses words on even one of their slides has to convince me there's an extremely compelling reason to do so.

Besides making sure no one's reading their talk directly off their slides or using super distracting frames and animations, you can try these tips for making presentations a success:

—Don't let students choose and organize their slides until their script and timing are complete. This helps keep the talk focused on the speaker, not the screen.

—If you plan to film the event, emphasize that students must have the rights to publish every image they use on the screen. The default should always be: share your own photos and short videos. Everyone has a digital camera they can use or borrow, today.

—Try having students create their slideshows using Google Slides. This tool is free, simple to organize, accessible anywhere there's Internet, offers real-time collaboration by team members in different locations, and makes it easy for a teacher to save and access all of the work on presentation day. Learn more at google.com/slides/about.

4. Learn it by rote

After these discussions, the real work begins.

We spend more than two weeks writing and revising the scripts for their talks, designing and critiquing slides, and rehearsing, rehearsing, rehearsing. I give students class time for both writing and memorizing.

Yes, memorizing. Every student is required to memorize and rehearse their complete talk until it's as seamless as it is engaging. Believe me: making my students memorize their presentation does not win me any "most popular teacher" contests. Quite the opposite!

But I still require it. Presentations are 10 times better when students have them committed to memory. And even students who feel extremely reluctant to memorize feel deeply empowered afterward.

When students invest the effort to memorize well, enough that they appear to be telling a story or holding a conversation, the entire presentation becomes both concise and powerful. Students polish their sentences until each one has an impact. They don't ramble. The act of memorization focuses the presentation on what matters most: connecting with the audience and communicating an important message.

Do students get on stage and freeze up? Do their minds go blank? Absolutely—but they're prepared for this. Instead of panicking or saying, "I forgot my line," my students are coached to forget the script and go into full-on storytelling mode. They know to ad lib. Tell an anecdote. Talk about the project to the audience just as they've talked to everyone else about it all year.

It works.

5. Make the tweaks

It's not enough to draft, edit, memorize and rehearse. We need an audience and we need familiarity to make an event successful.

My students practice their editing and communication skills through peer review of each other's talks, offering critiques to help each other improve. (We're able to do this because we spend the entire year creating a culture of trust.)

Then, we put the students on the stage. We turn on the spotlights and projector, set up the rest of the class as audience, and run a full dress rehearsal. It's tremendously helpful to know what it's like to be under the lights, to be managing the equipment at the same time as the presentation, and to know what to expect from yourself and your team.

At the end, we talk about how much courage it takes to get up in front of people to share something important, and we acknowledge that courage in each student who does it.

6. Prepare the magic

The students aren't the only ones who stay busy preparing for their final exam. I do a good portion of work behind the scenes to set things up.

Depending on their workload, you may consider involving students in these tasks as well:

—*Scheduling.*
This has been the biggest challenge of the entire project for my classes, since we're competing with final exams.

—*Reserve performance space.*
If you're using a school theater or auditorium, it's a good idea to request the space at the start of the school year and confirm availability well before the event.

—*Coordinate audio/video.*
For our presentations, we use spotlights, multiple microphones, a projector and screen, a video recorder and tripod.

—*Find a TED-style round red rug for the stage.*
(See "pageantry.")

—*Invite the community.*
Direct invitations go a long way toward fostering community connections. I encourage my students to invite their families, friends and other important people in their lives. Consider posting announcements for school staff and students, reaching out to administrators in your own district as well as neighbors, sending letters to local politicians, spreading the word among community leaders, etc.

—*Send press releases to local media.*
This includes metro and alternative newspapers, major and nonprofit television and radio stations, online communities/social media and popular bloggers. Seeing themselves in news coverage is tremendously exciting for students, and it en-

courages them to bring their best to the stage. *You can find a sample press release, including video, at 20time.org/pr.*

Remember—just like the projects themselves, it's crucial for press releases to focus on the audience and their needs. Pitch the event to editors as something that will attract their readers, viewers, or listeners. Show how the event benefits the community and inspires its members, perhaps even leading to community collaborations around the students' ideas.

7. Let go

Remember those unmotivated students? In every single academic endeavor I've ever encountered, a small percentage of students don't do the work at all. I've never seen a teacher be 100 percent successful with every student, all the time.

Not even 20time programs are immune. I've had students who gave a lousy proposal and didn't address the feedback they got from me and their peers. I've had students who didn't do their blog posts or memorize their elevator speech. Some talks were badly written, weren't properly rehearsed, or didn't engage the audience at all.

For the most part, I've learned to not take these students' non-participation personally, and to let go of trying to change them. But I never want to give up on students, especially those who are putting in the work. Those kids, I try to meet halfway.

Again, when a 20time presentation seems on track for failure, I check with the student or group to see what's going on that's making it hard to complete their work. If they're worried about performance, I tell them I've never seen a student who did the work have their presentation flop. Sometimes I remind them that the talk is a major part of their grade—not just for the project, but for the whole class. It's their final exam. If they don't do it, they could drop an entire letter grade.

I often talk about how, no matter what, the students are probably feeling a pull to tell people about the work that they've done. Even if their project didn't go as planned, they set an idea of their own into motion and put in at least some effort to learn what they could along the way. There's value in that. Sometimes more value than a "successful" project can offer.

I also remind myself about one of my favorite presentations, presented by students in my 2012-2013 class. At the start of the year, this group of girls hated the idea of 20time and detested the requirement of presenting their results to a large group. Eventually, they came up with the idea of teaching technology to senior citizens. They went on to organize and lead a successful class at a local senior center on how to use Facebook. By the end of the project, they were absolute converts, and their team was incredibly excited to tell as many people as they could. *You can watch their final presentation, along with several others, at 20time.org/talks.*

It's worth continuing to reach out and help reluctant students find their way to success. Just don't fall into the trap of pouring more effort into their project than they're willing to.

Surviving 20time — as a teacher

As you can probably guess, teachers who want to find a way to reduce workload should not lead a 20time program.

Even with good boundaries, this experience takes a lot of time to manage, from the opening letter to the last presentation.

I've learned to create systems to make it easier. For instance, I don't read every student's blog in detail. I just scan them to make sure they're on track. I also follow Alice Chen's model of a shared online form to see at a glance how teams are doing. *A quick video guide on how to create these forms can be found at 20time.org/blogcheck.*

Also, much of my evaluating and connecting takes place during the classroom day dedicated to 20time student work each week. I try to check in with every individual student during that session to make sure they're doing the work and to offer support where needed.

In addition, I make adjustments to my overall curriculum. 20time projects help meet the skills prioritized by Common Core in many ways, so most classes should find some flexibility in their syllabi. My English students, for instance, didn't read as much canonical literature as they otherwise would. Instead, they read a lot more nonfiction, and students wrote a lot more about their projects than they did about novels. That helped free up many hours while still allowing them to meet academic goals. It's different from what I learned in school, but the tradeoff is totally worth it.

I don't spend hours and hours in the evenings doing 20time work—unless I really want to. I often get joyfully sucked into my students' work. It's like recess for me. I want to be involved and go to events and watch my students thrive. It's an absolute pleasure.

I hope it's just as enjoyable for you.

A chance to shine

Congratulations! You now know *how* to run a 20time program. Here's a little more about why you *should.*

Students who don't do well on traditional academic assignments can bloom through this assignment. 20time is an opportunity for some students to create their own standard of success, because they have so much control over their work. Students who don't do well regurgitating textbooks can feel valued and find meaning from making something compelling or serving a need.

20time is a chance for "non-standard" kids to have a good experience in school.

I know that when people visit my school, they frequently comment on how articulate, poised and confident students are. Juniors and seniors who've completed 20time projects often cite their presentation process as helping them with public speaking. A few minutes in front of a group of peers or adults is no longer a big deal. Alumni come back and say this was one of the most meaning-ful experiences they've had.

I'm very confident that over the next 20 years, I'm going to keep hearing back from these students, and that a disproportionate number of them will have stepped into roles as successful business executives, community leaders and entrepreneurs.

Even better, I'm certain that some of them will be helping us truly solve the wicked problems of the world.

Chapter III
Fail Forward

I sold knives door to door one summer when I was in college.

More accurately: I went door to door one summer when I was in college, NOT selling knives.

Knocking on people's doors for hour after hour, day after day, and being disappointed almost every single time was an amazing experience. In fact, it's an experience I hope every single one of my students gets to do as soon as possible.

Why am I such a fan? Because diving into rejection and failure is an incredibly productive way to build tenacity, learn new skills, create new strategies, and get crucial practice in not taking criticism personally.

In education, I see a growing recognition that our experiences of failure are essential opportunities for learning. Messing up and learning from the experience is a far more powerful way to educate students than by having them get good grades on their tests. But while more schools are talking about these benefits, I don't know of many that truly celebrate students' failure. Instead, failing is seen as it always has been in Western education: something terrible. Getting a bad grade on a paper is bad news. Not getting into the science fair or the school play is even worse. But getting in only for your volcano to fail to erupt or your memory to fail during your big line? Worst. Day. Ever.

Unless you've been trained for this.

We need to change how we as teachers respond to failure, and we need to start coaching our students on how to respond as well. This doesn't mean we teach kids to strive for failure. When it occurs, however, we have to identify it as a very positive opportunity.

Reverse the pattern

For instance, most classrooms follow the model of having a teacher or textbook deliver information on how to solve a problem, and then let students attempt to use what they've learned to reach the solution.

Increasing evidence shows that we have this backwards, because when we reverse the usual pattern, students learn far better. For instance, Google offers a number of free online courses, including a class teaching people about advanced online searches. At first, instructors taught several search techniques, then sent students off to use the new skills and find certain content.

Later, the instructors tested the model in reverse. Students were sent hunting only to come back empty handed. They had failed. But the instructors followed up by teaching the new techniques. These students understood the lessons faster and more deeply than their traditional-learning peers, and when sent after the content for a second time, they reached it much more quickly.

Failure teaches us so much more than the familiar lecture-test model because the process has meaning and context. Our brains have something concrete to latch onto, instead of trying to make sense of an abstract solution to a problem we haven't experienced yet.

The lessons suddenly have an understandable purpose.

Set your students up to fail

When we embrace the possibility of failure and draw attention to what we learn when it happens, we help students learn to safely risk much more.

I believe that helping students be both risk-tolerant and experienced at managing their risks is one of the most important things we teachers can do. Yes, they may fail to achieve their risky goals, but they'll learn important information for future projects along the way. If they do make it, they'll learn that it's okay to strive for what seems to be beyond possible.

Consider an example from ancient Greek mythology of what happens when we don't teach about risk. To escape the island of Crete, the engineer Daedalus built wings of goose feathers and wax for himself and his son, Icarus. As they suited up, Daedalus warned his son not to fly too far upward, or the heat of the sun would melt his wings and he would plummet to the sea.

It's no surprise that Icarus flew too high, lost his wings, and drowned. Rather than blame teenage impulsiveness and hubris, though, I think we should note that Icarus had no chance to practice his flight or witness other people's failures in advance. He also didn't get to practice recovering from failure before the landing would be fatal. Maybe he'd have noticed the problem soon enough to fly lower, or he'd have some backup wax and feathers to fix the wings before hitting the water.

That's why, instead of telling high-performing students that they're geniuses, we need to burst their bubbles before they find themselves too high to safely fall. Help them shoot for the moon and navigate the inevitable failures along the way.

We also need to encourage students—especially the high performers—to work hard, even without a guarantee of success. And I don't mean any more hours studying content and striving for grades. I mean working at things that don't come easily to them. Every student is counting on us to teach them failure so they can learn to persist, to get dirty, to take risks, to fail without giving up, to dust themselves off, and to keep making and producing no matter what.

Done is better than perfect

Perhaps the best way to help students get comfortable with failure is to change our definition of success.

First, a nod to having high expectations. Everyone knows that the higher expectations we set for students, the higher they tend to perform. Don't be afraid to tell students who aren't giving their all: "That was a pretty good job, but I know you can do better." If a team has a challenging goal, and you believe they can achieve it, have confidence. Tell that team to go for it. Encourage them to strive. Put them in those tough situations and let them bring their best game.

Of course, telling students their 20time project has to end world hunger doesn't help anybody. That's the dark side of high expectations: perfectionism. All-or-nothing thinking.

There *is* a place for perfection in my classroom: on vocabulary quizzes and when using punctuation. But when working on projects that require creativity and innovation, I tell my students that the quest for perfection always leads to incompletion.

How many people do you know who will start a terrific project only to abandon it when they hit the first hurdle?

How many work and rework it dozens of times until the end result is worse than when they began?

How many creations don't see the light of day because the creator never thinks it's is good enough?

Too many, in all those cases. What we can take away from these all-too-familiar failures is this: Striving for perfection is the surest way to kill a 20time project.

Here's some ways to battle the perfection monster with your students:

—I have a poster in my classroom inspired by one at Facebook headquarters: "Done Is Better Than Perfect." I point to that poster probably three times a week.

—I also play song I recorded for my students using the very fun AutoRap app: "Failure is an option / Failure to deliver is not." *You can find this video at 20time.org/autorap.*

—When a kid takes a risk and fails, I point it out and celebrate their courage in aiming high. Students catch on quickly and start doing the same thing. We laugh with anyone we catch shooting for perfection instead. We honor each other for sticking with a creative work when the going gets tough.

—We end up with a class where everyone is biased toward action instead of perfection. My students know what they want their good, quality creative work to look like, but they understand that it will take many, many hours of ugly practice before it can shine.

Don't worry if it takes awhile to build this kind of culture with your students. Just like everyone fails in their first year of teaching, you'll get through the first stumbles, and you'll get better.

So will they.

Close that gap

One final thought on perfectionism from the radio personality and producer Ira Glass (*This American Life*):

Nobody tells this to people who are beginners. I wish someone told me. All of us who do creative work, we get into it because we have good taste. But there is this gap. For the first couple years you make stuff, it's just not that good. It's trying to be good; it has potential; but it's not. But your taste, the thing that got you into the game, is still killer. And your taste is why your work disappoints you. A lot of people never get past this phase. They quit. Most people I know who do interesting, creative work went through years of this. We know our work doesn't have this special thing that we want it to have. We all go through this. And if you are just starting out or you are still in this phase, you gotta know it's normal, and the most important thing you can do is do a lot of work. Put yourself on a deadline, so that every week you will finish one story. It is only by going through a volume of work that you will close that gap, and your work will be as good as your ambitions. And I took longer to figure out how to do this than anyone I've ever met. It's gonna take awhile. It's normal to take awhile. You've just gotta fight your way through.

Failure = creativity

Why does combating perfectionism matter for 20time programs? Because our entire goal is to encourage creative problem solving in our students.

We already know that extrinsic motivators (including competition and grades) lock our brains into "what-we've-already-learned-will-work." When we're given permission to test and fail, we're freed up to explore radically new approaches to the problems along the way.

After all, truly creative thinking requires three key elements, according to workplace change agent and author Daniel Pink.

—**We need autonomy**. Students need more freedom in what they learn and how they learn it. That means freedom to make mistakes and not reach their initial goals.

—**We need mastery**. Or at least the sense that we're moving toward it. As students see progress on their projects and realize their skills are getting better, their excitement grows, building intrinsic motivation. If they're expected to be successful from day one, they don't get to experience the joy of improvement.

—**We need purpose**. When students see that the learning they're doing has deeper meaning and helps others, rather than just pleasing a teacher or bringing in good grades, they're eager to do more. A strong purpose helps them sustain through disappointments, frustrations and any number of failures along the way.

For instance, in 2012-2013, I had a group of students who were incredibly excited about trying to break a world record. They wanted to host the longest-lasting barbecue dinner ever—a barbecue that would last for at least 48 hours.

The students contacted Guinness World Records, started making plans, and invested dozens of hours in the project. Then, someone read the fine print.

Due to liability issues, no one can be certified as a world record holder until they're at least 15 years old.

Guinness confirmed that they would not recognize the dinner, no matter how long it lasted.

The students were deeply disappointed. But even without the motivation of a world record, the team moved forward. They decided to hold the barbecue anyway and use it to help feed the hungry of Monterey County. That experience not only did more good for the community, the students found it far more meaningful than getting their names listed in a records book.

A world-class failure

That doesn't mean it's easy to turn failure into a positive, creative learning opportunity. Some disappointments can be simply crushing.

When you have students who don't believe they can recover from a major failure, tell them this story.

On April Fool's Day of 1976, 21-year-old Steve Jobs and a pair of friends started a tiny computer company called Apple. Nine years later, the company board fired Jobs over his strategy for boosting Macintosh sales.

Epic fail.

John Sculley, Apple's then-CEO, later shared regrets for the decision. The former Pepsi executive said he hadn't understood the need for visionary, risky, out-on-the-edges leadership for a company in the early stages of a new industry. In his experience as a competitor in a well-established field, Scully said, "you don't make mistakes, because if you lose, you're out."

An even more epic fail.

That could have been the end for both Jobs and Apple. Instead, Jobs dove right back into computing, founding NeXT, Inc. to develop and manufacture computer workstations for the higher education and business markets. In 1986, he also funded a small graphics startup corporation, spun off from the Lucasfilm computer division, called Pixar.

Ten years later, the Apple board recognized Jobs' leadership and vision. They purchased NeXT for $429 million and 1.5 million shares of Apple stock, and restored Jobs as an Apple leader.

What he learned as a result of that early failure helped Jobs recreate his old company as a world-changing pioneer in consumer electronics. Apple is now the largest publicly traded corporation in the world, with annual revenues above $180 billion. His ideas helped make millions of people's lives better and more delightful, allowing us to be more creative and productive in what we do.

Before his death in 2011, Jobs reached his goal of putting a "dent in the universe."

Not bad for such a world-class failure.

Chapter IV
Audience-Centered Learning

Inevitably, I have students who show up to my class on the first day of school telling me what they want to do for 20time. They're only missing one thing: who it's for.

"I've always wanted to write a novel. Can I write a novel?"

"Yes, a novel is a great 20time project. Start thinking about who your readers will be, so you can interview them before you begin writing."

"I like working with dogs, and I want to train some for my 20time Project."

"Great. Will they be companion dogs or working dogs?"

"I think companions."

"Cool. Companions for families, seniors, people with disabilities?"

"Probably disabilities."

Or...

"I always wanted to build a website."

"Good. What kind of website?"

"A website for teenagers."

"Better. You know that audience better than I do. Is this a website for all teenagers?"

"Um, a website for teenagers who want to raise chickens?"
"Yes. Run with it."

The power of the niche

What's so great about a website for teenagers who want to raise chickens is that it has a niche audience. Before the Internet, media producers had to reach the broadest audience possible in order to make up production and distribution costs. (I've seen reruns of MacGyver. Clearly, those producers were reaching for the lowest common denominator.)

Now, creators can afford to distribute their books, websites, infographics, podcasts, and videocasts to the exact audiences they're looking for. Instead of casting the net as wide as possible, they can target a narrow group of people with unusual interests.

For instance, each Thursday evening, a group of friends and I get on our computers and meet for a Hangout OnAir using Google+. (Notably, it's already Friday morning for Chris, the Australian in the group.) We broadcast a video conference talking about what's new with Google in education. Do a search for "Google Educast" to find us. Anyone in the world can watch us live or download the broadcast.

But most people don't.

Most people aren't interested at all in what's happening with Google in education. Most teachers aren't interested in Google in education. Even most Google fanboys aren't interested in Google in education! But there is a small sliver of people around the world who are interested enough to want to watch or listen to us talk for an hour about their favorite topic of interest.

Are we making money? No. But money is not the motivating factor in most creative projects.

We're motivated, in Pink's terms, by our **autonomy**. Our producer, Dan, gives us feedback and some direction, but for the most part, we decide how to run the show.

We're also motivated by **mastery**. Each show seems to get better and better. (Please don't listen to my shows from 2012. Not only am I probably recommending Google Reader, which is now gone, but I am also probably stumbling over my notes. I still stumble, but not quite as much.)

Finally, we're motivated by **purpose**—our audience. Each week, a few hundred people make the time to tune in and hear our show, and we get questions and comments from them. That keeps us going year after year.

Your students' audience is probably going to be very small for a very long time. You need to tell them that up front, and help them celebrate every audience member. The goal is not to reach the whole world. It's to reach a small but loyal group of fans.

I share some of the many recent success stories of businesses built on small target audiences with my students to show them where finding a small, loyal group of followers might lead.

One great illustration is Flitetest.com, which started out with a few Midwesterners who love RC airplanes. Their local community of RC geeks was quite small. However, with the power of YouTube, connected with a world-wide community of true RC geeks. Their YouTube page now has more than 175,000 subscribers, and they're able to make a living by testing model planes and posting reviews and tutorials online. Their fans are extremely loyal and constantly engaged in their work.

The camera manufacturer GoPro offers another nice example. Entering the cameras industry was a real challenge, given the huge number of much larger companies that can produce them much more cheaply. But GoPro targeted a niche market that the other companies hadn't tapped into: people who love adventure sports and want to document their activities. GoPro went public and transformed both the camera and extreme sport worlds. They're now one of the hottest technology stocks on the market.

Audience: Teacher, student...or better?

During my first five years leading 20time, I spent a great deal of time shifting projects from being teacher-centered to student-centered.

That was a fail.

One of the main reasons I love the 20time model is that it's important to have class time when the teacher is off center stage. This approach energizes and liberates many of my students (while confusing and terrifying others). I was committed to establishing a student-centered project, where my classes could take the lead, facing challenges and solving problems any way they saw fit. The results were terrific.

The problem was that I didn't take things far enough. A 20time project should NOT be student-centered. It should be *audience*-centered.

A student-centered project is one that focuses on the creator's needs and desires. An audience-centered or user-centered project focuses on the actual person who will use, experience or be affected by the project.

We develop this perspective through research on the actual people who will experience or be affected by the solution. This process should involve building empathy with them.

Those steps are critical if we want our students to take more ownership of their education. We need to show them that the goal is not just to impress their teachers or their parents or to feel good about themselves. They need to understand that they have an ability to affect the world around them—and they need to see the impact they can have.

Many of my students recognized on their own that their project should be audience-centered. A few went even further. Consider the group who decided to teach technology to senior citizens. Before they began solving all of the seniors' problems, the students took the time to assess where individuals were in their expertise and asked about their goals for using technology. The team adapted beautifully to the responses. Instead of a wide-ranging project teaching seniors about all sorts of technology, the students developed a program to teach Facebook skills in a classroom setting to help elders connect with their far-flung family and friends. They showed a commitment to both research and empathy.

Instead of hoping students will come to this approach on their own, I encourage teachers to make empathy a more structured component of the 20time program in their classrooms. After students identify what type of project they want to pursue, they need to identify the audience or user base. Then, they must interview potential users and empathize with them to better understand how to solve the problem. This part of the process is not only essential, it's a ton of fun.

There is still a place for student-centered learning in my classroom, just as there is still a place for teacher-centered learning and perfection. I like to think that the closer the learning goals are toward rote memorization and basic understanding, the more the work should be teacher-centered. As activities work their way through understanding into application, they shift to student-centered. But when we come to analyzing, evaluating and creating, we should make sure our lessons go beyond the classroom to focus on a real, authentic audience.

And that leads to why I don't call my students' 20time work "passion projects."

No one cares about your passion

Here in coastal California, we hear the inspirational phrase "follow your passion" somewhere in the neighborhood of every 15 minutes.

This isn't a good thing, because "follow your passion" is really bad advice. We don't need any more narcissists and navel-gazers. We need people prepared to engage the world where the pain points are and make a positive difference. And that requires people to go a step beyond the usual advice.

Here's what I tell my students: "No one cares about your passion. I'm glad you have a passion, but if it doesn't translate into something that's valuable to somebody else, it doesn't belong in a 20time project. If you want to learn the saxophone, and you're really passionate about it, that's great. Go do it. But not on my time. If you want to produce tutorials to help other people learn to play saxophone, or record music videos for people who love hearing young saxophonists, you've got yourself a 20time project."

I remember one student whose passion was to make money. We worked with that. He launched a web business that helped people meet their Internet needs while becoming profitable within a couple of months. Not only that, this student learned that one of the best ways to make money is through helping others. That's worth celebrating.

The key is that a 20time proposal has to have both a product (physical, experiential or digital) and an audience. Without both of these elements, it's just a chance for kids to mess around in the comfort zone of a private hobby. They don't have to actually engage with the world, learn about others' needs and desires, or wrestle with the big challenges of doing something with a larger meaning or purpose than their own pleasure.

That's not what educators are here for, and it's not what students need to take on wicked problems in the world.

Chapter V
The Learning Game

Every teacher and homeschooling parent I know struggles with making sure the children in their care receive an education that will meet the standards of their district, community and the waiting world.

Not surprisingly, innovative educational methods such as 20time can raise fears that students won't graduate with the standard skills and knowledge we believe they'll need to be competitive.

But you *can* incorporate project-based learning into your classroom or home-based curriculum without shortchanging your students along the way.

Assess without stifling

The first 20time question I get from students and parents is: "How are you going to grade this?"

This was one of the toughest questions my first year. The 20time project is a major component of a course where I'm required to measurably improve student skills and growth. That's usually achieved through the use of grades. But the whole 20time program is designed to counter the influence of extrinsic motivators such as grades. Focusing on grades undermines the culture of innovation and creativity that I'm trying to nurture with this project.

Students would be much more likely to play it safe by trying to determine what I view as successful or worthy of pursuit, rather than seeking merit within and among themselves. I could devise a rubric of what a good 20time project looks like, but I would invariably fail to include all of the possibilities of what could make a great one. Here's the happy medium I've developed.

—I only grade the *algorithmic*, or objective components of the class—the parts that demonstrate measurable achievement and work. Great blog posts, proposals, or presentations are mostly formulaic, so grading them motivates success.

—I grade the formal proposal as I would any other writing project with a specific rubric: on both style and substance. Is it on time? Is it complete? Does it answer the required questions? Does it follow the guidelines for written English?

—I grade the blog posts on a pass-fail basis. Were they published on time? Were they long enough? Did they address the required topic? Did they include publishable images?

—I "grade" productivity by intervening. If students aren't spending their project time actively and passionately working on 20time and making progress, we need to quickly adjust the project so students are working on something intrinsically motivating.

—I grade the end-of-year presentation as I would any other student presentation. Did it meet all of the required elements?

All four elements are important to 20time and students' overall grades, but grading them doesn't risk shutting down the innovation and creativity needed to create a compelling project.

Learn as you go

Not long after I'd started offering 20time, a fellow teacher wanted to bring the program into her classroom. She asked: "Should we have students project their learning outcomes?"

I had to read the question a few times before I could comprehend it.

At that point, I required my students to list "learning outcomes" right in their proposal. Learning outcomes are the goals we expect to accomplish from any given project: gaining expertise in a particular software, improving interview skills, figuring out how to run a small business. For me, learning goals are right up there with safety in my list of classroom priorities.

I felt as if she had asked, "Should we have students breathe air?"

I soon had the opportunity to attend a seminar with Yong Zhao, author of *World Class Learners: Educating Creative & Entrepreneurial Students*. Assuming this advocate of project-based learning would support me, I repeated my colleague's question to him.

He paused, then responded: "Do you think Steve Jobs asked himself, 'I wonder what I would learn if I invented an iPhone?'."

His response made my requirement for students to predict their learning seem absurd. Of course Jobs wouldn't ask himself what he would learn in the process. He simply dove in—and learned an enormous amount along the way. And that's exactly what I need to let my students do during 20time.

Learning is obviously a natural outcome (and goal) of 20time, and I will mention my academic requirements for the project as needed

Nevertheless, I no longer ask students to focus on what academic standards they expect to improve or what knowledge they expect to gain. I want my students' predictions and attention centered on how their audience will benefit from their work.

Tie 20time to academic disciplines

At some point, we may all agree that learning should not be broken up by silos in the form of separate departments and classes. Human brains work best when integrating information across multiple disciplines. Students who get to work with math, computer programming, chemistry, art, Spanish and world history all at once instead of in separate periods throughout the day are much more likely to retain the information they encounter and develop proficiency across the board.

Until that approach is integrated into Western education, I think it makes sense for 20time to deliberately incorporate learning goals from the class where the project is happening.

My earliest 20time students took the program as part of an English class. It made sense for writing to play a major role in their 20time program. Of course, students who wanted to focus on projects that were literary in scope were free to do so. But the formal proposal, weekly blogging, and scripted and edited final presentation helped ensure that all of my students, regardless of project topic, were building the language skills they'd need to thrive in future classes and careers.

Today, I teach technology. I've scaled back some of the writing requirements, and I require that all projects have a computer programming component. One student might design an Android app to help students learn guitar, while another could develop a branching-logic algorithm to help customers at the local SPCA choose the training classes that are best for them and their dogs.

What about other subject areas?

—Let's start with world **history**, which I taught for several years. The most rigorous assignment I gave in my career was to these classes: I asked them to publish a Wikipedia article on a history topic of their choice. Each student had to dive deep into Wikipedia's strenuous article submission guidelines, meticulously cite their sources, and scour their research for relevant, accurate information. The army of volunteer Wikipedia editors are severe and exacting. Only a few of my students' articles actually survived the process. This is one example of how an authentic project could meet both 20time goals and history class goals.

— **Science** teachers, you have it easy. You've been doing 20time projects since the very first science fair. (By the way, Google has a killer science fair at googlesciencefair.com. Goodbye, trifold poster boards and papier mâché volcanoes. Hello, dynamic websites with video and animated data.) Try setting these up as 20time affairs with targeted audiences and elements of entrepreneurship, and see how creative your students become.

— **Art** and **music** teachers, your shows and recitals are more great examples of project-based learning at work. Bringing the formal 20time project guidelines into the mix can encourage students to think beyond self-expression and explore how their art can impact audiences and the world.

— **Math** students can do 20time as well. Let them choose projects that require simple or complex data analysis, explore mathematics history, apply their math skills to financial models, or encourage deep learning in a challenging mathematical area.

— How about this for a project: **Foreign language** students could partner with native speakers and work together to solve a global problem — giving students an authentic, meaningful reason to learn each other's language.

And so on. Let us know how you make 20time work for your students — and you — at 20time.org.

20time and Common Core

I teach at an independent school exempt from public education mandates, but I pay close attention to the implementation of Common Core standards in public school systems.

These standards establish goals for students across the United States, but do not attempt to define the means teachers can use to help their students achieve those goals.

The Common Core State Standards Initiative, the body responsible for generating the standards, is emphatic on this point: "The Common Core is not a curriculum. It is a clear set of shared goals and expectations for what knowledge and skills will help our students succeed... Teachers will continue to devise lesson plans and tailor instruction to the individual needs of the students in their classrooms."

I believe this approach to public education offers tremendous opportunities for teachers who want to incorporate independent, student-determined projects into their classes. Traditional state standards, especially those introduced by No Child Left Behind, often limit teachers' possibilities for fostering independent student work. Common Core allows teachers to increase the rigor of the curriculum while creating space for project-based learning.

If a teacher designs and structures a 20time program with specific Common Core goals in mind, then it can be instrumental in helping students reach those goals. In fact, many of my colleagues in public school classrooms have concluded that giving students the autonomy to pursue ambitious, independent projects might be *the best way* to meet some of the priorities of the Common Core.

Examples of some of the Common Core standards that 20time can help achieve are:

—communication
—speaking and listening
—presentation
—collaboration

—problem-solving
—research.

In any given project, students have the opportunity to master formal writing style and tone in their proposals and presentations, work closely with peers and mentors, use short and long research projects to answer questions and solve problems, and to develop research skills, all while expanding their "domain-specific vocabulary" and using technology to present and publish their work. All of these skills directly address Common Core standards.

Here are a few more specific ways that 20time and Common Core standards go well together:

—English Language Arts
I didn't tell my English students this, but 20time projects in my classroom were really writing projects. Starting with the formal proposal, students were constantly writing about their experiences. Their final presentations, based on their carefully written and edited scripts, were some of the best writing I saw from my students all year. Why? Because students were writing about work that was meaningful for them, and they were writing for an authentic audience. They knew that the broader community would see them present this work, and it would serve as a public narrative of the projects they were so heavily invested in. What better way to encourage students to bring their very best to meeting the Common Core standards?

—Technology
Technology in education must involve more than transferring the contents of textbooks to glowing rectangles with animated icons. It's about empowering students to be inspiring creators and authentic problem solvers using the most effective tools available today.

20time helps students go beyond educational apps and games, providing opportunities for real-world applications. Students can go deep, learning to use technology to create websites, publish books, produce apps, build communities and more. All of which meet the vision of Common Core.

—Mathematics

There are two ways to teach students about 15% interest rates. *Use the properties of exponents to transform expressions for exponential functions. For example, the expression 1.15t can be rewritten as (1.151/12)12t ≈ 1.01212t to reveal the approximate equivalent monthly interest rate if the annual rate is 15%.*

I remember this challenge from high school. I was told to demonstrate my understanding of the concept by solving a series of problems. I recall flipping to the back of the textbook to check my answers to see if I was correct. Mind-numbing work. Then, there's the 20time approach. My colleague John Stevens uses this to teach personal finance skills to his teenage math students in San Bernardino, California. Using the same math skills standards, students can create a video that conveys the dangers of holding a balance on a credit card with an annual rate of 15%. Or they can build a web application that calculates how quickly a credit card balance can grow, given a 15% annual rate and a cardholder who only makes the minimum monthly payment. These activities not only provide meaningful, authentic context for abstract math problems, they provide purpose by showing real-world impacts. Students no longer solve such problems to pass a course. They solve these problems to help themselves, their families and their loved ones make smart decisions about their finances.

With a little creativity, 20time projects can be used to help achieve any number of Common Core goals in any number of academic disciplines. Let the guidelines for your classroom outcomes be a framework that inspires more innovation by your students—not a straitjacket that keeps them from learning about and exploring their world in meaningful, effective ways.

Chapter VI
Ready For Launch

Now you know how and why to run an effective 20time program. But are you ready for launch?

The hardest part of 20time for us educators is making the commitment to do it. It's a decision that requires courage, because it takes us well away from the familiar, top-down model of traditional classrooms. It requires tremendous amounts of time and energy as we challenge ourselves to keep pace with our students and their creative vision. And it calls for a leap of faith, asking us to give our students the power to fail—while trusting that, with a little guidance and encouragement, they'll find the way to succeed beyond our dreams.

The good news is, almost all students do find a way to succeed. Even if their own projects don't pan out, just the experience of being surrounded by (and taught by) fellow risk takers, innovators and visionaries helps young people become more future-ready.

The same is true for us as educators. I guarantee that if you decide to offer a 20time program, not everything will turn out as planned. You will catch students rolling their eyes. You will hear from worried parents. Your video projector will fail on the night of the big presentations.

Do it anyway.

Because your students need someone who believes they can succeed at a major endeavor of their own.

Because there are thousands of people whose lives are waiting to be touched by your students' work.

Because we need to set our young people free from the traditional box of exclusively teacher-focused, test-based education systems.

Because students need opportunities like 20time to go deep and make a real difference in their community and in the world.

I encourage you to use this book as a launch pad for your own 20time program. Learn from my mistakes! Then share your experiences and draw on the resources of the community of life-long learners at 20time.org.

I deeply believe that the work we do as educators to prepare our students for the future is the most important work we can be doing today. We are all on this rocket ship to that future together.

I look forward to hearing how the journey goes for you and your classrooms.

And when you get stuck along the way, remember: Done Is Better Than Perfect.

Appendix I
Success Stories

It's hard to start a major project if you don't know what it will look like in the end. Here are a few examples of successful 20time projects and how they evolved along the way.

The Book Blog

Maria Stanica told us about her work in between promoting her site on her Twitter, Tumblr, Goodreads, and Instagram accounts.

Maria Stanica's sophomore-year 20time project spreads her infectious enthusiasm for books to the online world, one video blog post at a time

"Getting my first 100 subscribers was really hard," Stanica says. "But then it started going up by 100 every week."

By the end of the year, the daughter of Romanian immigrants—both math teachers—had filmed 65 videos and attracted more than 1,100 subscribers.

"It's been amazing," she says. "I go to school and I'm just me. And then I come home and I have all these tweets and messages on Goodreads about how they love my videos, and I'm so eloquent and mature for my age, and 'you're such an inspiration to me. It's really touched me and impressed me and humbled me to think that I've affected someone in that way."

Besides finding time on top of school and softball practice to research, draft and film her blog, Stanica says her biggest challenge was getting used to the camera.

"In the beginning, I felt so awkward sitting in my room just talking to myself," she says. "The first few (video) descriptions were all: 'I'm so sorry I'm awkward!' Now it just feels like I'm talking to a whole group of friends, one at a time."

Stanica turned that initial awkwardness into an advantage. For her early videos, she included blooper reels with sped-up, high-pitched audio, adding to the series' charm.

Otherwise, she says the project was fairly simple. She uses her laptop's camera, free iMovie editing software, and lighting from "the sun or a lamp in my room."

Her key to success? Making content she knew her audience would like, but she still cared about.

"If you're not passionate, your audience can totally tell, and it will fail."

The benefits of doing a video blog on books were clear right away, she says, from broadening her reading list to improving her speaking skills.

"I'm more confident in my ideas and opinions, now," Stanica says. "I've become less afraid that people are going to disagree and not believe what I believe."

And she received plenty of support, both at home and from the Booktube community of YouTube book reviewers.

"It's a two-way street," she says. "A lot of it was me tweeting and promoting and commenting on other people's videos. And my parents are really, really supportive as well. They watched every single one of my videos, liked them, and gave me constructive criticism."

For those considering a 20time project, Stanica says, "it's very, very important to target things you love and you're really going to enjoy doing. When they say 20 percent of your time, it's not a joke."

What's next for her, now that the official project is over?

"I've decided I'm going to continue to make videos, grow my audience, do what I'm doing," she says. "I've made too many friends—and I'm really proud of where this has been going. I definitely want to see where it goes."

YouTube: youtube.com/user/bookloverwriter13
20time blog: mariaprojectbooktube.blogspot.com

Cooking up success

In fall 2013, York School sophomores Tiana Alexander and Soraya Levy realized they had a delicious idea for a 20time project. Let's see where it took them.

Tiana Alexander and Soraya Levy got the inspiration for their upcoming 20time project while visiting a local amusement park.

"We saw all these Instagram accounts scribbled on the walls of the roller coasters," Tiana said.

"We thought, we both enjoy cooking. We could do a cooking blog on Instagram," Soraya said.

The two started talking about dishes they liked, and the field trip turned into a major brainstorming session. By the end, they'd decided to launch a food blog called "Cook That."

The plan was to tackle a cooking project each week at one of their houses, then photograph their work and post it on Instagram.

The friends spend a lot of time figuring out recipes, including how to fix those they "messed up on," Soraya said.

"We only had one major mess-up," said Tiana. "We just can't cook gnocchi."

"We've tried!" Soraya agreed. "It just doesn't work."

The blog's numbers are strong, with 47 posts and 1,745 followers as of October 2014. The most popular photo has 404 likes—a pear tart.

Of course, that's far short of the goal in their 20time Proposal: 500,000 followers for the blog.

"Mr. Brookhouser told us to come up with moon shots, and 500,000 stuck," Soraya said. "So we harassed our friends a lot and got our classmates to follow us. We looked up hashtags like #chef and #culinarystudent and liked all the pictures under the tags, and then they would look at us and then follow us."

"I don't think we expected to get 500,000," Tiana said. "We were really excited about getting 1,000. [When it happened], we were baking a cake and refreshing the page every 10 seconds. We'll hit [500,000] eventually."

Just as exciting as the numbers are the response.

"On every post," said Soraya, "we get a couple comments like, 'Good job, guys!'"

"'You should go to culinary school,' super nice things like that," Tiana said. "I didn't expect the feedback to be so positive. A lot of people say, 'Wow, you guys are only in high school?' That's a real compliment."

The best response so far? An invitation to be featured in a local cooking magazine. (They said yes.)

Besides the gnocchi, what was their biggest challenge?

"Definitely the photography," Soraya said. "That was the largest learning curve."

Tiana agreed. "We were both pretty confident in our cooking skills beforehand, and cooking is mostly just following instructions. But photos involve a lot more problem-solving. The food could look really good, but once we took a photo, we'd say, 'Oh, God, that doesn't look appetizing!'"

Since the two usually start cooking around 4 pm and don't finish for four or five hours, they often have no natural light.

"The other food accounts we're following [on Instagram] have studios," Soraya said.

"We have my kitchen floor and back yard," Tiana said with a laugh. "There'd be one of us lying on the floor with a camera, the other holding up a white T-shirt and two table lamps."

While the cooking and photography were done at home, Tiana and Soraya used their 20time period at school to plan recipes, researching them online and combining what they found into a single, workable approach.

What have the benefits been?

"Getting to eat the food!" Soraya said. "It's so satisfying to be able to eat this product you worked so hard on. And since we got to try making all these dishes, we're more experienced cooking weird things."

Tiana said she's grateful for all the chefs who follow the blog and send comments from around the world.

While both now enjoy photography, neither wants to pursue the food industry as her main career.

"But it's a good ability to have," Soraya said.

"Yeah," Tiana agreed, "we'll be really popular in college."

Even after their final presentation in May 2014, Tiana and Soraya have continued cooking and posting—just not every week.

The students have more schoolwork as juniors, Soraya said, "and we don't feel as much of an obligation to update, since it's not part of a class."

That's been a good lesson about self-motivation. Despite their strong drive, without deadlines or accountability, the two only get together about once a month, Tiana said. That's led to some advice for future 20timers:

"Pick something you're really interested in," she said, "so it doesn't become a chore. Don't just throw something together. And do it with someone you enjoy!"

With fewer posts and less time spent finding and liking other Instagram cooks, the young chefs have seen a slow-down in new followers.

"We'll keep it going, though," said Tiana. "We know now that it's possible, and do-able."

"And fun," Soraya said.

"It's definitely fun," Tiana said.

Instagram: Instagram.com/cookthat
Tiana & Soraya's final presentation:
  youtube.com/watch?v=3mpnVRFsLRU

Building For The Future

Riley Gaucher and Phillip Boureston's ambitious sophomore year 20time project taught them far more than just architectural skills. Here's their story, in Riley's own words.

When your teacher tells you you're going to attempt a project entirely of your choosing, the endless possibilities are both extremely exciting and completely overwhelming. But even more overwhelming is learning that this project will require 20 percent of your time throughout an entire school year. I don't remember one time in my life where I've planned six months in advance, let alone the 10 that encompass a school year. So I was naturally daunted when, the week before my sophomore year at York School, in Monterey, California, I received a letter from Mr. Kevin Brookhouser describing the project I outlined above. That letter from my English teacher impacted my entire year.

I was not new to the concept of inquiry-based learning. The school I attended from kindergarten to 8th grade emphasized projects based on students' interests. But this project was an entirely new level of freedom. I love the ability to research my own interest and find a creative idea to present. But when Mr. Brookhouser gave us his one requirement, that we had to make something—produce a product that could in theory be sold—it didn't help me narrow down my ideas.

This was a problem. I'm great at coming up with ideas, but I'm also tremendously indecisive. I have trouble deciding on what flavor of ice cream to eat, let alone a multistep, year-altering project. I had some vague concepts, but none of them seemed right. This is where The Bad Idea Factory came in. A Bad Idea Factory simply involves generating as many horrible, dangerous, stupid ideas as possible. Though it may seem counterproductive, this process usually results in one or two ideas that turn out to be not so bad after all, or it leads to new, better ideas. Our class covered whiteboards with hundreds of bad ideas, ranging from "drop pennies off high stuff" to "be a pirate" to "write a book sideways" to "set some stuff on fire." Through this process, I decided on planning a fictitious city, Sim City style.

Now I needed a partner. We had the choice of working alone or with up to 2 other people, and I knew I didn't want to work alone. I eventually partnered with Philip Boureston, my friend since 4th grade and my frequent collaborator on school projects. After Philip agreed to work with me, I pitched him my idea. He wisely talked me down into designing a house; specifically, an environmentally friendly house.

Once Mr. Brookhouser approved our project, the next step was to find a mentor—an adult who could provide expertise in the area of our project and support us if we had issues. Mr. Brookhouser suggested a local architect, a friend of his and the designer of the Science Building at our school, Ken Scates. Mr. Scates actually has an office just down the hill from York, and he readily agreed to be our mentor. He is an expert in green building, and coincidentally, was teaching a class at our local Community College on the basics of green design. In our first meeting, he recommended several strategies for designing our house, and showed us a cool system for laying out the rooms. In a green house, the orientation of rooms is the most critical aspect, because it dictates which rooms are heated most effectively by the sun.

So Phillip and I messed around with a couple of different arrangements before selecting the one we liked. Then the challenge became to finalize the floor plan. This consumed an inordinate amount time, and we literally covered an entire notepad with variations on the same design. Finally, we were ready to start working on our final product, a 3-D model of our design.

One of the major decisions we faced early on that Mr. Scates helped us solve was what software to use when creating our house. Initially, we wanted to use professional architecture software, but this cost over $3,000. Instead, Mr. Scates suggested SketchUp, a free program we could download from the Internet that allowed us to created 3-D objects of any shape and size.

We started creating our digital model, but our final exam, a live presentation of all our work, was fast approaching. We quickly realized there wasn't enough time for our ambitious plan, which called for landscaping and extensive interior design. So we focused on one of Mr. Brookhouser's favorite' mantras, "Done is better than perfect." To have something we were proud of, we had to make sacrifices in scope. We confronted the impending deadline by working harder, working more efficiently and accepting that not everything we wanted to accomplish was feasible. Instead, we strived to do the best with what we had.

The final aspect of the project was a five-minute oral presentation on the process we undertook to create our product. Mr. Brookhouser called this the "Best 5," as in the best five minutes of our lives. Over the course of a weekend, Philip and I wrote endless drafts, at times throwing away the entire script. Finally, we had a presentation (a tad longer than five minutes!) that truly showed how much work we had put in. This step allowed us to bring together our entire 20time experience and demonstrate how much we had grasped and accomplished.

By the end, I'd learned a myriad of architectural concepts and the basics of eco-friendly design. However, these were the superficial benefits of the 20time project. While I didn't break my habit of procrastination, I did manage my time better, considering I had 20 percent of a school year to allocate. Philip and I overcame distraction, difficulties and disinterest while resisting the urge to play basketball instead of work.

Though it may sound cliché, I discovered that when I explore what I love, I'm more engaged, invested and have a more rewarding experience.

Due to the multi-faceted nature of the 20time project, I've learned how to interact with professionals, developed superior organization skills, and discovered how to generate creativity. I am sure to use the presenting tips, speaking skills and writing prowess in both the near future of college and in any career I end up having.

I am thankful to Mr. Brookhouser for helping me realize the benefits of dedicating a large fraction of my time to one goal, one product. Because the true lesson of the 20time project is to be happy with what you've created and realize that "Done is better than perfect."

Riley & Phillip's final presentation: 20time.org/talks

A Teacher's Perspective

Kate Petty teaches high school English in southern California, and runs a 20time community site at 20timeineducation.com.

People ask me what I like the best about 20time in my classroom. I could say it's the individualized learning that takes place, or the attention to goal setting, or the reflection.

But, honestly, you want to know what drives me to do it every year?

It's the amazing relationships and growth fostered throughout the project. Over the past two years, I have seen students form professional relationships with mentors, create full-fledged business enterprises with their "Shark-Tank" ideas, and grow up before my eyes as they come to understand responsibility and what it means to have others truly depend on them.

For instance:

At our Community Pitch two years ago, I had a mom come to me with tears in her eyes to thank me for integrating the 20time project into our class. She explained that her 12th-grade son, Cory, had a rather distant relationship with his father during high school. But for his 20time project, Cory decided to learn how to take care of and maintain his car. This mom told me that for the past four weeks, Cory and his father had been out in the driveway every Saturday working on the car and re-establishing their relationship.

During her final speech at the end of the 20time project, a student named Natalie showed a website she'd created for her family. Her mother, descended from a close Eastern European family, had died early in Natalie's life. Natalie had called her maternal grandmother and asked if she would teach Natalie the family recipes. Every Saturday night for three months, Natalie went to her grandmother's house and learned how to cook all of the delicious foods her family held close. Natalie created a website with the recipes and pictures of the meals for the rest of her family to use when needed.

When I first introduced the project, Tom had a very hard time. He started rocking back and forth at his desk with his hands covering his ears, he was so distraught. WHY was his teacher asking him to come up with a learning goal of his choice, when he wouldn't even be graded on whether he accomplished it or not? But he persevered. Tom decided to use this opportunity to break away from his father's photography business, where he was an apprentice, and begin his own company. Talk about great timing! He did so at the same time many of his fellow classmates needed their senior pictures taken. Tom ended up creating a pretty lucrative client list during that semester.

My favorite story comes from my own daughter's first-grade classroom. Her teacher, Mrs. Parsons, decided to try a "genius hour" with her students. (Genius Hours follow a similar to that of 20time projects, inviting students to take the lead in their own learning experience.) Mrs. Parsons requested donations of unused sports equipment from her students' families and received a nice supply of cones, balls, hula hoops, carpet samples, and more. She then asked the fifth graders to assist her class for an hour, creating games with the random equipment. As they rotated through the stations of equipment, each group came up with a different idea for how to use them for having fun together.

So, when you ask a 20time teacher WHY we lead these projects, you'll have different answers from each of us. This was mine.

Appendix II
Letter To Families

Here's a sample of the letter I've sent home at the start of the year for all of my 20time program students and their families. Feel free to draw on this in your own communications, or download a copy at 20time.com/letter.

Dear Students and Parents of the York School 10th Grade Class,

I hope you all had an adventurous and energizing summer. I'm writing to introduce myself and let you know a little about one of the unusual projects we'll be taking on this year in English III.

I'm a Google-certified educator who started teaching at York in 2002. I'm dedicated to future-centric learning that prepares students to tackle the major global challenges of the 21st century in meaningful ways.

My favorite booster rocket is the 20% Time Project. This major learning assignment spans the entire school year, somewhat akin to a thesis. The project gives students the opportunity to deeply pursue a creative interest they would otherwise not experience in our academic program at York.

Before I get into the details, let me explain why we ask students to participate in this activity. Over the past 20 years, more and more educational research has shown that the role of teachers needs to shift away from the industrial model, where a teacher lectures from the front of a classroom while students are supposed to sit quietly, consuming the information for later disgorgement on written tests.

Rather than acting as a "sage on the stage," many pedagogical experts say teachers should play the role of a "guide on the side." When students play a more active role in how content and knowledge are acquired, they're better prepared for the creative, flexible, self-led roles of the future. As guides, teachers can provide resources, ask questions, and make suggestions that help students stay on track and achieve real success.

There IS still a place for lecture, and I will still play "sage on the stage" at many points in this English course. But the 20time project will be a chance for your student to experience student-centered learning.

How does 20time work? Here are the seven core elements:

1. Brainstorming
At the start of the year, students begin brainstorming ideas for projects they'd like to devote 20 percent of their class-

room and study time to over the course of the year. Students may work alone, but I encourage them to work in small teams of up to four students.

The goal is to envision a project that will involve a completed product at the end of the year. It could be a physical product, such as a graphic novel or a balloon that takes photos from the stratosphere. It could be an organization, such as a tutoring pool or a webhosting business. It could be a digital project, such as a short film or video game or web series. Students will quickly move from this idea phase to the production phase.

2. Proposal

Once students and teams have an idea of what they want to pursue, they begin writing formal proposals to "pitch" their project to me and the rest of the class.

Proposals must answer the following questions:

—What is your project?

—Who will work with you on this project?

—Who is the audience/user base/client base for this project?

—Why is this project worthwhile?

—What PRODUCT will you have to show at the end of the year?

—What expenses will be involved in your project, and how will you cover them?

—What equipment will you need and where will you get it?

—What is your timeline for completing (or launching) your project?

3. The Blog

Each cycle (school week), every member of every team is required to write a public blog post discussing their progress. They write about what happened over the past cycle, what they learned, what challenges they faced, and what they anticipate in the future. Each blog post must be at least 150 words, written in Standard American English, and contain a related image that is posted without infringing on any copyright.

Students fill out a simple form that links to their post.

4. Mentors

Each student or team must seek out an adult mentor who can help guide and inspire them on their project. I hope parents and families will draw on their circles of community to help students find an appropriate mentor.

The mentor is encouraged to offer advice, provide informal leadership, and follow the blog(s).

5. 20time Days

Throughout the school year, I set aside one class day each cycle for students to work on their projects. In some cases, projects can only be worked on while a student is off campus. In those cases, students document their time spent on weekends or afternoons, and use our scheduled 20time class time as a tutorial period, meeting period or writing period.

6. The Final Presentation

At the end of the year, each team will show off their work by delivering a five-minute presentation with visual aids to students, teachers, and community members. These talks will be carefully written, choreographed, memorized and rehearsed to produce the best presentation they've ever given. The TED-style presentations will be delivered and recorded in the Theater—I hope you'll join us. It's always a powerful, moving, inspirational night.

7. Assessment

Many students and parents understandably ask me how I'm going to grade the 20time project. I try to de-emphasize the grade because extrinsic motivators tend to discourage the innovation and creativity I'm seeking from in this project. I want students to be inspired by the project itself, not by the grade they're going to get on it.

(Read Daniel Pink's book <u>Drive: The Surprising Truth About What Motivates Us</u>, for more on this. You can get a taste of it by watching Pink's 2009 TED talk, in which he argues for giving employees more autonomy in business. The book explains why the same principles apply to education, and provides much of the foundation for the 20time program's design.)

That said, I do assess students throughout the year on the algorithmic (objective) elements of the project. A significant portion of their English grade will be dependent on the following elements:

—**The Proposal** Is the proposal on time, and does it address the required questions appropriately?

—**The Blog** Are the posts meeting the required length and addressing the required topic? Are they posted regularly and their forms submitted on time?

—**The Product** Are students successfully moving from idea phase to production phase? Will they have something to show at the end of the year?

—**Productivity** Are students spending their 20time hours actively and passionately working on their project? If not, we need to quickly adjust the project so they're working on something intrinsically motivating. This is less objective, but if I see students not being productive, I will intervene.

—**Final Presentation** Does the presentation meet all of the required elements?

That's it. That's the 20% Time Project.

What if a project is a failure?

In this class there is a place for perfection. Vocabulary quizzes and sentence mechanics come to mind. The 20time project is no such place.

The world's best entrepreneurs embrace failure, and I ask my students to adopt this mentality too. (Read *Wired* magazine's January 2010 issue for a great summary of modern thought on the topic of "failure.")

The only truly failed 20time project is the one that doesn't get done. I want students to strive to deliver and present a successful product at the end of the year, but I don't want the quest for perfection to lead to an incomplete attempt. I want students to follow the advice plastered on the wall of Facebook's headquarters: Done Is Better Than Perfect.

This policy doesn't work in all environments. I wouldn't want to see this poster in the dentist's office or the parachute packing assembly line. But for creative projects where innovation and learning are the goals, I find this approach compelling.

If students feel that their projects are a failure, I want to hear about it. I'll ask what they've learned about it. (For more on what we can learn from failure, watch Kathryn Schultz's TED Talk: "On Being Wrong.")

To put this point simply, I tell students: don't strive for failure, but don't be afraid of it either!

If you have any questions about anything, don't hesitate to contact me.

I can't wait to be amazed, surprised, and inspired by the innovative projects this year's sophomores will produce in 20time.

Sincerely,
Kevin Brookhouser

Appendix III
How To Build A Bad Idea Factory

1. Get colored markers. Lots of colored markers.

2. If you have whiteboards in the classroom, use those. If not, get a bunch of butcher paper and spread it out on tables or the floor.

3. Tell students that their first job is to come up with the worst year-long project ideas they can think of in 20 minutes. "Keep it PG-rated, please!"

4. Their second—and more important—job is to fill up the space they're given with ideas, written or drawn using as many colors as possible. Sketching an idea is often better than using words.

5. Tell your students that if they notice an average or good idea along the way, they definitely need to write it down, too.

6. Set a timer that everyone can see. Shout: "Go!"

7. Encourage students to keep markers moving across the board. When kids get stuck with nothing bad to write, tell them that it's okay to write something that's not so bad. "This can also be the Boring Idea Factory."

8. Join the fun and write down some of your own bad ideas.

9. When the time is up, allow students to present their favorite bad ideas to the class. Celebrate the worst with equally bad prizes, such as an old sock, an empty water bottle, a broken pencil.

10. After the worst ideas are presented, ask students to transform some of those bad ideas into good ideas. I promise: you'll all be surprised and delighted by the results.

Appendix IV
The Proposal

Here is the template I provide students for their project proposals. Feel free to download a fully formatted copy at 20time.org/proposal.

20time Proposal Template

[Date]

[Team Members' last names]

Proposal: [Title of project]
  [Subtitle that helps describe the project]
  [Full name(s)]

Summary: [Brief introduction to the project.]

Needs and Opportunities: [Explain the problem you have noticed that needs to be solved with a project like yours.]

Audience / Clients / Users: [Explain who will benefit from your project. How will you be able to access them for an empathy interview?]

Timeline: [What is your monthly timeline for this project? I want to see a list of deliverables with deadlines. You may find that the timeline needs adjustment during the course of the year, which may be fine. Check in with me if you do need to make changes.]

Product: [What is the actual product you will come up with by this Spring? It may be made of atoms or bytes, but you must have something to show. I'm not interested in just seeing a bunch of great ideas at the end of the year. I want to see *things*.]

Reality Check: [Moonshots are encouraged, but even moonshots need budgets. What equipment are you going to need? What other capital expenditures do you anticipate, and how will you meet them?]

Conclusion: [Wrap it up. Why are you fired up about this project? Inspire me to support you, and give me a great reason to approve your project.]

Here's a sample of what I would consider a successful proposal.

Proposal: International Pen Pals
An exchange of language, culture, and lifestyle
Terri Typist and Ernie Emailer

Needs and Opportunities
In many ways, Americans live in an isolated society. Most of us are only familiar with the communities where we live. Although it is true that the Internet and social networks link together people with different backgrounds, many aspects of life in other parts of the world remain a mys-

tery. A basic knowledge of the various cultures of the world is an essential tool as we move forward in the 21st century.

This project seeks to break down the cultural barrier between our society and other parts of the world. What's more, since we believe a lack of understanding is almost always the cause of mistrust or fear between two individuals or two cultures, we hope this project can play at least a small role in educating others about how we live, and conversely, help us learn more about the life of students and youths in other countries.

Audience / Clients / Users

Our goal is to write a series of letters to 10 to 15 different high school age students living in different countries around the world. We will swap stories about our different communities, schools, and customs. Hopefully, this small group will share what we learn, increasing the number of people who can benefit from this enterprise.

In this project, we would also like to embrace other languages and overcome language barriers that separate cultures. Since both of us are currently studying Spanish, our plan is to include some students from Spanish-speaking countries. With this group, we can practice writing letters in Spanish while our pen pals can practice English by writing to us.

It will be fairly easy to interview people about our project, since the letters essentially consist of a series of interviews we will share at the end of the school year.

Timeline of Deliverables

Sept. 1	Proposal
Oct. 1	Make contact with 3+ potential pen pals
Nov. 1	2 letters written
Dec. 1	12 letters written
Jan. 1	20 letters written
Feb. 1	28 letters written
March 1	36 letters written. Maybe a video chat?
April 1	44 letters written. 3-4 video chats
May 1	50 letters written. Present journal

Product

At the end of the year, we will have a collection of all our letters to and from the pen pals. We will create a short publication of these letters, along with summaries of each pen pal and what we learned about his or her culture, language, and daily life.

Reality Check

This project will require very few expenses. We are planning on using an online site to send the majority of the letters to pen pals through e-mail. Therefore, a computer and Internet access will be required for this project, which will not be an issue. If we decide to exchange any physical items, there may be postage costs. We will keep these costs to no more than $50 per month, which we can cover through our income from babysitting and yard work.

Conclusion

We have a feeling that this project will be both engaging and educational. We're expecting to learn so much about the cultures and lifestyles of our pen pals, including small details unknown to most foreigners. We're excited to start writing letters and learning more about students in other countries: what they like to eat, what their favorite sports are, what their dream car is. The possibilities are endless, and we can't wait to meet some new people and share what we learn.

Appendix V
Recommended Reading

I am indebted to the following books and authors for their extraordinary insights. The influence of their research and the importance of their impacts on the 20time program cannot be overstated.

Daniel Pink
Drive: The Surprising Truth About What Motivates Us

A.J. Juliani
Inquiry & Innovation In The Classroom: Using 20% Time, Genius Hour, and PBL to Drive Student Success

Chris Anderson
The Long Tail: Why the Future of Business is Selling Less of More

Peter Brown, Henry Roediger III, Mark McDaniel
Make It Stick: The Science of Successful Learning

Carol Dweck
Mindset: The New Psychology of Success

Yong Zhao
World Class Learners: Educating Creative and Entrepreneurial Students

Appendix VI
Guide to Online Resources

Each of the following websites has been invaluable for me and fellow educators as we engage in project-based learning and the development of future-ready classrooms. I encourage you to dive in and explore the many tools and community resources available.

20time.org

The companion website to this book. It's a great place to show parents, administrators, colleagues and students exactly what the 20time program is all about—and how to bring it into their own educational experience. Watch videos. Download templates and resources. Read the blog. Get inspired. And spread 20time.

20time.org

Kevin Brookhouser

My home base. Here's where you can find out what keynotes, events and trainings I can offer for you or your organization, plus in-depth resource links and videos to classroom and technology tools.

kevinbrookhouser.com

20-Time In Education

A terrific collection of resources, case studies, interviews, videos, ideas and community support for educators bringing the benefits of project-based learning to their classrooms.

20timeineducation.com

The Future Ready Schools Summit

Produced by EdTechTeam, Inc., Future Ready Schools Summits are held at sites around the world to connect educational technologists and experts with educational communities eager to create future-ready classrooms.

futurereadysummit.com

Genius Hour

If 20time and Genius Hour were kids, they'd be best friends. Join some of the best Genius Hour teachers in their playground of ideas, resources and connections here.

livebinders.com/play/play?id=829279

iLead+Design

This summer camp based in Monterey, California brings high school students together for a two-week community action experience, where they work in collaborative teams to identify community problems, investigate opportunities, and design and deliver innovative solutions.

lyceum.org/ileaddesign

Techsmith

This software company's screencasting program, Camtasia, allows teachers and students to create amazing images and videos for the classroom and beyond. I can't recommend them enough.

techsmith.com

Appendix VII
Follow These 20time Leaders

There's a terrific, growing community of educators focused on making 20time successful in their classrooms and beyond. Find more of these leaders at 20time.org/teachers.

Troy Cockrum
Great thinking, examples and effective guides for educators on 20time projects and teaching in general.

cogitationsofmrcockrum.blogspot.com

Juan De Luca
The first Google Certified Teacher in Mexico, the first Google Education Trainer in Latin America and part of the first cohort of Apple Distinguished Educators in Mexico, Juan works around the world helping schools assess their technology needs and develop strategies to enhance teaching and learning practices with digital tools.

juandeluca.com

A.J. Juliani

A.J. offers terrific help convincing administrators and parents to support 20time for your students. His site provides excellent arguments and classroom guides for project-based learning.

educationismylife.com/designing-20-time-in-education

Joy Kirr

Joy has a great sense of how to encourage choice and inquiry in her students' classrooms. She helps inspire and guide fellow teachers through the #geniushour community online.

geniushour.blogspot.com

Denise Krebs

Denise offers Genius Hour inquiry-driven projects in her middle school classroom. Her blog, which details their progress throughout the year, is essential reading for project-driven instructors.

mrsdkrebs.edublogs.org

Karl Lindgren-Streicher

Karl is one of California's top leaders in effective technology integration in the classroom. Visit his site to join the conversations and view the models he presents in his high school classes.

about.me/LS_Karl

Kate Petty

Kate leads 20time in her high school classroom in Mission Viejo, California. Don't miss her online support center and guide to integrating 20time into classroom curriculum.

20timeineducation.com, thetechclassroom.com

Oliver Schinkten

Oliver says the real point of project-based learning is helping. Dive into his thoughtful site to deepen your understanding of why 20time in the classroom really matters.

ComPassionBasedLearning.blogspot.com

John Stevens

John, an educational technology coach and community leader, teaches high school in Upland, California. He's the author of *Flipping 2.0*, founder of #EdCampPS, and part of the Apps In Class (appsinclass.com) team. Join his community at @Jstevens009.

WouldYouRatherMath.com, fishing4tech.com

About the author

Kevin Brookhouser has been obsessed with computers since he was 12, pulling all-nighters programming games for his friends on an Apple IIe.

He is Director of Technology at York School, a trustee of The International School of Monterey, and the Student Agency Specialist at EdTechTeam.

He earned his master's of education degree at Lynchburg College in Lynchburg, Virginia, and is a Google Certified Teacher, Authorized Google Education Trainer, Microsoft Innovative Educator, Common Sense Media Educator, National Association of Independent Schools Teacher of the Future, and University of California Certified Integrated Course Developer.

Kevin lives in Monterey, California with his wife, Beth, and son, Sam.

CPSIA information can be obtained
at www.ICGtesting.com
Printed in the USA
FSHW020955070720
71936FS

9 781502 305244